This is a timely and provocative study of the living patterns, attitudes and educational needs of various minority groups in the United States. With an exceptional balance between urban and rural problems Dr. Charnofsky provides a sensitive view of our various sub-cultures of poverty. Such knowledge, he contends, is necessary before teachers can begin to make education a more meaningful experience for poor children.

Approaching his subject in a clear and fresh way, the author steps away from the standard books on poverty and education in his major themes:

- The "powerlessness" that pervades the personalities and life styles of the poor prevents them from succeeding in our educational system.
- It is the system itself that perpetuates this feeling of powerlessness.
- Before success in education can be achieved, the children of the poor must begin to feel the power that comes from self-confidence, self-awareness, and group identification.

Indicting our schools' practices, Dr. Charnofsky offers an humanistic approach to education—to the achievement of full human potential and power—for the poor with concrete suggestions for teacher education, teacher roles, and curriculum with built-in flexibility as the keynote. Dr. Charnofsky concludes by broadcasting the exciting new power that is emerging as the poor and culturally different "do it for themselves."

EDUCATING THE POWERLESS is unique both in its authentic presentation of the plight and stirrings of our many American sub-cultures and its vital connection of the theory of humanistic education with our gravest educational problems. It offers the reader new concepts both of our society and the role of education within it.

Educating
The Powerless

Stanley Charnofsky

San Fernando Valley State College

Wadsworth Publishing Company, Inc.   Belmont, California

L. C. Cat. Card No.: 70 —
154808

Printed in the United States
of America

1 2 3 4 5 6 7 8 9 10
—75 74 73 72 71

Preface

Formal education as it has evolved in our schools is supposed to pass on the values, the heritage, the accumulated knowledge of the community. But how can this be done when the community has become communi*ties?* When the world has shrunk, and culture becomes so influenced by a jet ride or a picture tube? When there are so many people with such diverse life styles that *the* heritage of a community becomes a misnomer? The people of this country are becoming slowly, sometimes painfully, aware of cultural diversity, and they are learning to accept it and even to live with it next door, across the street, in the market, at work. Why then are the designated agents of progress—our schools—among the last to recognize, in their offerings, the diversity and the pluralistic nature of the children and the families of America? Why are our educational programs continuing to direct their energies toward a mythical central culture that does not exist anywhere? And why do our schools thus continue to be the agents of degradation and shame for so many youngsters who are made so acutely aware of their difference from the "norm"? In a word, with diversity all around us, why do our schools continue programs which render large segments of American children *powerless?*

I am concerned with powerlessness. No other book that I have found has been willing to grapple, in any extensive way, with that phenomenon. No other writing approaches schooling for the culturally different through the thesis that, largely *because of* their differences, the different are powerless. And further, *because of* their differences, they are made to feel inferior, unable to learn, not a part of the school, outsiders, humiliated, lost. Many books still advocate changing the child. That represents a continuing belief in the inferiority of that child's life style, and I believe that it is antithetical to the avowed purpose of our democracy. I believe that our *institutions* must snap to; they must be tooled up for diversity; they must embrace difference as the essence of our heritage; they must exalt our diverse children as magnificent citizens of our diverse nation.

To be sure, there is progress, and educational programs are adapting and adjusting. Colleges and universities are leading us into new experimental ways of structuring and ordering the learning-teaching processes. We are trying to recruit members of different cultures into the field of education in the hope that they can be meaningful and relevant to their own people. And yet, many of our programs cannot get beyond the notion of training workers to fit into the system that presently exists. As a result, many black people, for example, have only been able to become teachers if they reject (or lose) the cultural aspects of their blackness. Little play is given to the concept that both our educational structures and society may need massive overhauls if they are to go on in harmony, and that education may need not only to reflect society, but to lead it.

The present, actual society is largely a hierarchical one with the dominant white-skinned, middle-class culture at the top and the dominated, mainly darker-skinned, so-called lower class cultures at the bottom. The result of that arrangement is a diffuse, pervasive, psychologically enormous message being sent to the bottom by the top that those at the bottom are somehow basically inferior. The message implies, in my estimation, one irresistible conclusion: those at the bottom are weak and helpless, unable to effect change, and *powerless* to alter their lowly position.

So we come to the themes of this book: (1) The powerlessness that pervades the personalities and the life styles of the under-groups of America keeps them from success in our educational system. (2) It is the nature of the system itself that perpetuates that feeling of powerlessness and not something basic in people. (3) Before success in education can be experienced, children of diversity must begin to feel the power that comes from self-confidence, self-worth, a sense of security and place, the uplifting quality of group identification, and the salutary effects of becoming aware of the value of one's own ideas and feelings.

And so with the writing that follows I shall attempt to explore the system that exists, to examine some changes that might be taking place, and to dream a little about what could happen if we only set our minds and our hearts to it. . . .

I began to write down my ideas and feelings after going through some "mind-blowing" experiences trying to work with teachers and potential teachers of culturally different children. At that time, I decided that unless I could make my writing something more than the logical, ordered, paragraphed, outlined, summarized, footnoted, technical, and inquisitorial textbook that you are used to, you would not be likely to read it. In any case, if the writing were stuffy, you would probably (as would I) turn off early in the game and complete it only as an assignment, if at all.

And so I have tried to write what follows, not for colleagues and professors, but for the students, the teachers, the learners, the ghetto workers, the paraprofessionals and aides, the people who interact together on America's newest frontier: the frontier where the culturally different confront the America that is dominant. The book deals with schools and learning, but it also deals with neighborhoods and communities and life styles and social movements and cultural history.

This is not a how-to textbook. It does not give the reader the lists of strategies to employ or the techniques to use in teaching people who are culturally different. It does not do those things because it is wedded to the philosophy that the teaching-learning process is a highly personal thing. *You* can facilitate another's learning and growth if you are: (1) all-together with yourself, (2) alert to and appreciative of *his* life style and essence as a unique human being, (3) tuned in to diversity as a positive and not a negative force, (4) sold on the growth potential of people, and (5) convinced that curriculum is personal and evolving, and cannot be externally and remotely imposed.

Yes, it can be hoped that your own personality will be opened to new values and new awarenesses through what follows, so that then the application of *you* to the learning-teaching encounter becomes the stimulus to successful education for America's minorities.

I consider the topic of this book more than desirable for all teachers or teachers-to-be; I consider it indispensable! You may disagree with my hypotheses or my conclusions (however tentative), but the subject matter itself is the chief crisis of our age. It may be the key to the survival of interaction between people as it is now known.

Join me by reading on. And I encourage you to read creatively. Because, as I think about my ideas, I am more and more aware of their creative limitations. And as I think about my writing, I realize that it is only motivational, not exhaustive; anecdotal and representational, not authoritative and conclusive. It remains, then, for the reader to pick up on whatever germs of ideas he finds herein, and to fly wherever his expansive imagination may take him. The beautifully diverse children of America today *need* your wildest dreams if their own are to have any hope of coming true.

I am indebted to several people for helping me to order my writing so that my emotions did not completely erase a sense of logic about my presentation. Thanks to the following (who criticized my manuscript) for keeping me straight: Dorothy Westby-Gibson of San Francisco State; A. Harry Passow of Teachers College, Columbia; Donald Carr of the University of Oregon; Garth Blackham of Arizona State University; Arthur Pearl of the University of Oregon; Edward Ponder of the Institute of Developmental Studies at New York University; and Dick Greenberg (who argued with me).

Contents

When an American says that he loves his country, he means not only that he loves the New England hills, the prairies glistening in the sun, the wide and rising plains, the great mountains, and the sea. He means that he loves an inner air, and inner light in which freedom lives and in which a man can draw the breath of self-respect.

(Adlai E. Stevenson, speech in New York City, 27 August 1952, during the presidential campaign.)

Part One

Life Styles
of the Poor

Chapter One

Urban
Ghetto Living

In Watts, a supervisor in a job placement and rehabilitation center once told me that the middle class didn't even have the same concepts about what made a good worker—nor about a great number of other things—as did the people he counseled with daily. He offered some examples.

An equal opportunity employer notified him that he needed 15 workers who would be trained on the job and who would be paid $100 per week. The employer would want to interview for the openings in a couple of days, and could the supervisor assist by soliciting for potential employees? The supervisor did this, briefing some 20 possible workers as to dress, personal grooming, and brief historical background of the company and their philosophy of labor-management relations. When the actual interviews were held, the supervisor found himself explaining to the employer the view from inside the ghetto.

The employer asked to interview, first of all, candidates with "stable job records," and the supervisor was forced to tell him the following anecdote: "Willie doesn't have a stable job record by your standards. If he did he would be working right now and not looking for your job. But every Thursday morning for the last three years, Willie has helped old Mr. Hancock unload his truck, and Willie's gotten $10. That's $10 on the line, not two weeks later, and Willie's *never* missed a Thursday. I'd consider him a pretty reliable worker. . . ."

Another employer asked if a candidate was a good driver (most worthwhile employment opportunities are many miles from Watts and the public transportation in Los Angeles is notoriously poor) as he did not want to lose a worker because of accidents or a forfeited driving license. The supervisor explained: "Where do you live? In suburbia? O.K., how often does a cop drive by your corner? Once a week? Every three days? Can't you fudge on a stop sign now and then? Every seven minutes a cop drives by our corner outside. If we roll on through, we got a ticket. We're good drivers if we've still got licenses!"

The employers who recruit in the ghetto advertise equal opportunity, but they mention nothing about the inequality of *access* to that opportunity. In an open competitive job market, the ghetto dweller is likely to lose to his more acculturated Anglo countryman, for few employers are currently willing to choose the less qualified candidate.

But why are ghetto dwellers consistently less qualified for the better jobs than their mainstream counterparts? Where does the access to skills, training, technical ability, and knowhow fall short? And how can access to equal opportunity be enhanced so that within the present economic and political framework the ghetto dweller can compete?

It is simplistic to assume that formal public education is in itself the answer. Yet our schools are everywhere, and they are ready-made agents for change—but only if they can prove themselves pertinent to the lives and needs of the urban slum child.

Anthropologist Oscar Lewis has attempted to examine the life styles of the people who live in poverty. He indicates the magnitude of the problem of reaching those people through the traditional means of education. To know, beforehand, the behavior patterns of any given population is a necessary but not a sufficient condition for influencing such a population in the classroom. Other factors are vitally related, such as the value system of the teacher, the regulations of the school (as handed down by the power structure of the society), and the existing employment market (students of urban schools very quickly *tune in* to those learnings which have significance to their daily lives).

Mr. Lewis writes: "The culture of poverty is not just a matter of deprivation or disorganization, a term signifying the absence of something. It is a culture in the traditional anthropological sense in that it provides human beings with a design for living, with a ready-made set of solutions for human problems. . . ." (13)

The people who live in poverty often develop a "culture of poverty," Mr. Lewis points out. It is a different way of living, totally alien to the expectations of the middle class and its institutions.

He further states: "The dominant class asserts a set of values that prizes thrift and the accumulation of wealth and property, stresses the possibility of upward mobility and explains low economic status as the result of individual personal inadequacy and inferiority." (13)

Sending Messages to the Poor

Our educational system must confront the probability that our schools reflect the notion of the dominant class, that poverty is the natural ". . . result of individual personal inadequacy and inferiority." Are our schools indeed in the business of reinforcing such a belief? Perhaps it is true that the urban school, offering little to rectify the historical neglect of the rural-background child, is actually contributing extensively to further decay.

Today's urban slum child peers out at an awesome and confusing world holding minimal promise for him. Mass communication constantly reminds him, in tantalizing, lyrical, limerical, and colorful displays, of his body odors, dirtiness, shabbiness, verbal inadequacies, physical differences, environmental limits, and overwhelming poverty. Prior to the age of television, the differences, while certainly present, were not so readily communicated to the poor. That the poor manage

to have television, and that they spend so much time viewing it, points
to their compelling need for personal escape and a chance at a fleeting
encounter with the involvements, the goods, and the goodies of the
dominant culture.

But television is only one brush with the larger society, and an
unreal one at best. In the everyday world of seeking identity and a
niche, the poor of this land are apt to deal mostly with the bureaucratic and mechanistic world of government agencies. These agencies
take the form of everything from the punitive, uniformed "headbreak-
ers" of Harlem, to the condescendingly probing social workers in a
dozen big city ghettos. It is a remarkably vertical relationship, with
the poor always looking up—for assistance on the one hand, and for
leniency or mercy on the other. The interesting thing is that it has
always been a matter of the poor asking for whatever the establishment would be willing to give. It was seldom a case of "rights" or
of justice. But the scene is shifting. . . .

While sociological literature discusses the matriarchal nature of
ghetto family life, the itinerant husband, and the endless series of
"uncles" or male transients who briefly take his place, it is not at all
clear that this pattern of living, especially today, prevails. In statistical
terms relief rolls are high, but in actual contacts with people in poverty it becomes apparent that the social workers are viewed with
great suspicion and that much is concealed or withheld from them.
In fact, practical experience discloses that the husband, under the
present system, is often unable to find work and is receiving unemployment compensation; but while living with his family, this is all he
receives. He has discovered that if he moves out, his family can also
receive county welfare aid. So he "moves out" whenever the social
worker is in the neighborhood but lives in for all practical purposes.
While this operation is typical of poor people in general, it has been
categorized as a lower-class Negro behavior syndrome, and has been
called by many a Negro problem. Workers in the ghetto areas, however, have labeled it a Negro solution (and quite a resourceful one)
to the problems imposed upon them by the stratified culture. Thus,
it is not at all certain that the ghetto husband and father is absent as
much as the figures would indicate.

The above is another example of the slum dweller's involvement
with the bureaucracy of government. Its intricacies dominate his life
and challenge his ingenuity. The child grows to adulthood remarkably
versed in the ways and means of center-city survival. But again, his
techniques are solely concerned with coping with existing situations.
A larger consideration is whether people of poverty see the present
pattern being totally demolished and replaced by a new, creative,
enhancing pattern.

Some students of contemporary American urban living have introduced an hypothesis of power as the overwhelming factor in substandard living. People who have no power (or comparatively little) to control their lives must necessarily suffer from a tarnished self-image. (This hypothesis will be examined in more detail in the section on the Psychological Health of the Poor.)

The traditional mode of motivating people who feel powerless has been to hold out the carrot, as it were—to hold out the key to the kingdom of middle-classness. The sanctity of the kingdom is carefully controlled by insuring that the key is obtained by obeying all the rules of those who live there. . . . Thus the kingdom is kept intact, its members become homogenized, and the differences between them and those who do not reach for the key become overpowering.

In the above transaction, the community and the school have been relatively successful. We have managed to engage the brighter students, to alienate them (sometimes inadvertently) from their original group, and to entice them into the kingdom by the promise of acquisitive success. But the vast majority of ghetto dwellers remain uncalled and unreaching, powerless and ultimately hopeless. The larger society decides to whom and to how many the right of choice will be offered. This is quite different from the notion (supposedly "basic" to American ideology) that choice and freedom are the rights of all.

Those who subscribe to the power hypothesis point out that dominant cultures classically have been quite jealous of their own modes of living and seldom if ever have volunteered to alter them, to relinquish their power, or to admit "contaminating" cultural influences into positions of control. Thus, when power will not be given, it must be taken—hence the conflict pervading our social order today.

"Take" power becomes a rallying cry with which vast numbers of less privileged citizens can identify. The urban ghetto dweller begins to see himself having some semblance of identity as he finds others uniting with him in their new common purpose. This mood of identification has spurred the growth of such aphorisms, for example, among the black militants, as "black is beautiful," and "buy black, be black."

Small wonder, though, that comfortable, middle-class America reacts with fear and vindictiveness to the stentorian cry for "black power." The reaction, more often than not, has been an appeal for "democratic power," for careful and prudent legislation to curb the advance of lawlessness and radicalism. The entire notion of "taking" power, the way it has been articulated and implemented (and, certainly, distorted by many who see a new, equalitarian society emerging *only* from the charred remains of this present one), has frightened the typical American who, growing prosperous and more contented

Power and Power-lessness

in his highest-in-history standard of living, has had only the most superficial contacts with people of poverty. Mr. America, in many instances, cannot believe the contentions and demands of the urban ghetto dweller. He sees no signs of the serious human problems that the news media report are motivating minority members to revolt and destruction. Often, he has been *through* but not *to* center-city for years.

Recently, a group of teachers going through an in-service program to assist them in their teaching of urban poverty children took a field trip to a small, severely depressed black ghetto in a city near Los Angeles. A young high school senior asked if she could spend the day with the group, as she was doing a research paper on the subject and lived in that city. During the experience, the girl confessed to the teachers that, although she had lived only seven miles from the area all her life, she had never been there before—her parents would not have allowed her to go this time except on the condition that she "stay in the bus and close to the teachers."

That the American middle class has been largely unaware of the festering sore in its midst is evidenced by the intensity of its current reaction to the cries of pain coming from the wound. When the poor cry out in the language of the streets, the larger society reacts with its own cries: "Crime in the streets!" "Race riots!" "Law and order!" "National Guard!" "Riot control!" "Unlawful minority!" "Malcontents!" But to the minority (Floyd McKissick, former National Director of the Congress of Racial Equality, has emphasized this as his perception of the situation) such cries from "the establishment" amount to one incontrovertible fact: suppression. . . .

Children of the Slums

Our middle-class children grow up learning to cope with the interplay and byplay of all the electronic devices, modes of communication and transportation, and types and amounts of goods and services that they desire and can commandeer. The maturation process is, generally, a sophisticating process; one of guiding and conditioning the young person into (as Eric Berne put it) the "games people play." (3) These games, this learning to manipulate the environment and to shape it as needed, are the logical accretions of the complexity of our culture. All people do what they feel they *must* do in order to enhance themselves and their lives.

The children of poverty cope in a different way, yet they too are attempting to enhance themselves and their lives. Theirs is a world of immediacy. There is less psychological manipulation and more physical manipulation. Abraham Maslow describes a hierarchy of human needs, ranging from the basic physiological motivations to the more subtle and often camouflaged psychological ones. (15) He states that until the needs for food, warmth and comfort, safety, sexual gratification, etc., are met, the human organism cannot begin to search for esteem, love, self-fulfillment (actualization), and the higher aesthetic needs. Children in slums have coped, not primarily to "save face," "look good," "be popular," or "be accepted," nor have they struggled for fulfillment or to actualize their human potential. Rather, they have endeavored to "be safe," "shake the fuzz," "fool the man," "make out." It appears to be a reasonable hypothesis that the notion of fulfillment, in the sense of reaching for one's human potential, has not been the pervading motivation in the lives of powerless people. Instead of such "growth motivation," people without hope must concern themselves with "maintenance motivation." Their daily lives are absorbed with the struggles to maintain physical and emotional adequacy.

A remarkable phenomenon of recent years is the explosion toward selfhood of the urban black. The writing of James Baldwin, (1,2) Claude Brown, (5) Ralph Ellison, (10) Warren Miller, (16) Stokely Carmichael, (7) and Eldridge Cleaver (8) have influenced a growing trend toward identification with an ethnic and racial milieu. Brown, in his *Manchild in the Promised Land,* writes of the incipient pride in Harlem, in the late 1950s, in the beautiful "black chicks" who paraded by on the streets. Black was really "sumpin' else." To be black was to be beautiful. And this growth in self-acceptance has burgeoned and indeed exploded. As black children begin to feel the forces of the large world tugging at them, their resources for struggle and for resistance seem greater. Their identification and their self-concepts are reinforced by a movement, a good feeling of belonging to a larger cause. Thus their motivations begin (and have begun) to change; the higher-order needs begin to emerge; the psychological needs cry out for satisfaction. The old adage that revolution occurs only after progress has already been felt appears indeed to be applicable.

But I do not wish to suggest that the slum child now feels the need to cope with the typically middle-class problems of getting ahead, self-esteem, etc. This might be the case if examples such as the drive to identify black as beautiful did indeed pervade the country's urban ghettos. But, while certainly vocal and influential, the movement is still selective, touching the lives of only a portion of those people of differing life styles. Even among the black population (and certainly among the Mexican-American, Puerto Rican, poor whites, and diverse other groups) there are hard core poverty people who live untouched by the power that an uplifted self-concept can give.

Children of the poor grow up, typically, feeling unsure of themselves and their worth, put-upon by the enormous ogre of society, and helpless to control or to guide their own lives. Thus, in numerous instances, the view from the slums is conditioned by the realities of daily need, pervaded by the immediacy of coping for existence.

There is growing evidence that the ability of children to be successful in our present American school system is predicated upon a healthy personal outlook and a relatively positive self-concept. That these positive self-concepts do not exist among our urban ghetto children—and therefore neither does the typical academic success pattern—has been illustrated through several pieces of recent research.

Morse studied 600 pupils in alternate grades from third to eleventh and found that third graders showed high self-regard; from that grade on, self-concept decreased significantly until the eleventh grade, and even then 44 percent of the eleventh graders wished they were someone else. (17)

Webster and Kroger studied adolescent blacks in the San Francisco Bay area in three integrated high schools. Over 300 youngsters were interviewed by questionnaire, and results indicated, among other things, that (1) blacks with white friends displayed higher total self-concept scores than those without white friends, and (2) blacks with white friends held higher vocational aspirations and higher expectations of vocational attainment than those without white friends. (19) These latter findings may have some critical implications for non-integrated or ghetto schools.

Further research has established a link between adequate concept of self and academic achievement in school. Bruck, at Michigan State University, measured the self-concepts of 300 pupils from the third through the sixth grades and also from the eleventh grade. His findings showed a significant positive relationship at all grade levels between self-concept and grade point average. (6)

Wattenberg and Clifford studied 185 Detroit children over a two-and-a-half year period, starting with their kindergarten experiences. Among other findings, they discovered that measures of self-concept and ego strength among kindergarten children predicted future reading achievement. In other words, children with more positive self-concepts in kindergarten were found to attain higher reading levels over the time span studied. (18) They also found that measures of self-concept combined with mental tests are better predictors of a child's potential than are the mental tests alone. (18)

Brookover and Thomas also sought to uncover a relationship between self-concept and school achievement. In a study reported in 1964, they sampled 1050 seventh grade students. Their findings indicated a *significant positive correlation between self-concept and performace in the academic role.* (4)

The findings cited above, and others, have led one researcher to comment, "The purpose of education is to produce more adequate people; a way to producing more adequate people is to improve their concept of self." (9)

But who are these urban dwellers with deflated senses of their own worth? What people in our land of opportunity do not find true the old European immigrants' alluring tale that "the streets are paved with gold"?

The major groups living in the urban slums who seem to be characterized by powerlessness and depressed self-concepts are black and Puerto Rican (in the eastern U.S.), Mexican-American (in the western U.S.), and poor white. The last-named, while large in number and in the intensity of their poverty, are not ghettoized in the same way as are the racial minorities. American Indians, while a minority, are not at present living in urban centers in great masses, although this too is beginning to change.

We shall discuss briefly each of the above-named urban ghetto-dwelling groups in order to work backwards along our hypothesis that the urban poverty culture has a genesis in most instances in a rural life style that comes under constant and massive attack when its constituents leave the rural areas. The urban slums represent people who are culturally different from the middle-class American norm. How are they different? What forms do their differences take?

The urban black man is really a transplanted rural black man. **The Urban Black** Since the early 1920s, when immigration from Europe was halted, the menial urban tasks required of underskilled laborers began to go to blacks. The deep South rumbled with the rumors of that "hebbin to dah north." The grandsons and granddaughters of America's slaves began to fill up the low-rent areas of Baltimore, Philadelphia, Detroit, Chicago, New York, Boston. . . .

Their outlook was rural and their color was black. The city, deperate for their labor, welcomed them but kept them at arm's length. (One black student recently told a white school administrator, "What do you think, man, that we made the ghettoes? We didn't put all those black kids in Jefferson High—you did!") The notion of ghetto began to be well-defined, and the cultural styles which developed there were replete with the characteristic poverty syndromes and the unique life styles of a people with slave beginnings, rural habits, and an underdog outlook.

Larger America has not been able to appreciate that there is a difference between a poverty life style (which seems to have similar characteristics throughout the world), and the culture of American blacks. The latter is, among other things, a complex of unbelievable psychological deprivation and the myriad coping mechanisms such deprivation has created.

Black people today are not slaves in the technical sense, but their self-confidence, their expectations of success or mobility, and their motivation are all very certainly influenced by that slavery that once was. Ghettoized as blacks have been, the acculturation process Americans have come to expect of immigrant groups did not occur. Deflated as they have been and cut off from an old world heritage of family success or technical skill, they have been unable to "learn the language and master the system." Restrained as they have been by their color, their rural and nonmechanistic backgrounds, and the extreme prejudice of the dominant cultures of America, they have remained, for all practical purposes, rural black people living in an encapsulated urban setting. The poverty incumbent upon their locale and their condition is a further complicating factor. . . .

As the black rural child enrolled in the urban school, the kinds of tasks he was asked to master were basically urban-inspired and urban-necessitated. For most urban American children, such tasks were well-suited (although sometimes badly taught anyway). But for rural black children who looked towards lives in an urban ghetto surrounded by others of rural black heritage, the tasks seemed meaningless, unrelated to their lives, distant, and even oppressive. Television and mass communication have penetrated the ghetto and changed some of that—there is now more of an awareness of the way such tasks can be used in American society—but that has managed to add to the sense of futility of black children who, knowing now what they *should* do, feel more demeaned than ever that they cannot.

The typical urban Negro child of today, as he moves into the city's schools, comes from a family whose father has yet to feel the power and pride of a true breadwinner. Black men (as well as Puerto Ricans) are still often unskilled, at the bottom of the occupational hierarchy, and not infrequently unemployed. In the hardest of times, women could earn more than their husbands. This compounded an already debasing situation for the black man, and his solution was often to leave. There is improvement in this picture as the job market expands for dark-skinned people. Yet the prestige of a profession or a white-collar job still largely escapes black men and, as a result, escapes the expectations of their children. (Recent findings have indicated that the best predictor of a young person's college attendance is not his grades or test scores, but whether or not his parents went to college.)

The depression of the 1930s had enormous impact on blacks in cities, as they were the least skilled and the first fired. Poverty over-whelmed their lives. Patterns of money usage began to emerge from those hard times, and the present-day notions of putting off gratification and saving for the future have been slow to invade the black life pattern. He had been thoroughly conditioned to scarcity, to paucity. Like others with uncertain incomes, he developed wasteful and bombastic spending habits. When he made it, he spent it; after all, it might not be there tomorrow. Any windfall brought on a gaudy display of opulence, even if tomorrow might find it all gone.

The gap between some of this socially conditioned behavior and the behavior of the middle class widened. And as it widened, other patterns of behavior and difference became more obvious. Helplessness before the awesome intricacy of the American system guided the rurally nurtured black to rely upon external forces. Superstition and humility developed as natural crutches in the face of a deep sense of powerlessness. (The Congress of Racial Equality, white volunteers in the Deep South in the middle 1960s, began to realize that as long as they were working to help the black man, the black man would not take the leadership role. "Yassuh, Mr. Charlie," could only be stopped if all the Mr. Charlies stayed home, and so the CORE volunteers did.) The result of not feeling able to cope with the system has had a circular effect, and the failure to try has kept blacks inexperienced and ultimately unskilled and backward. They live in the city but remain unacculturated to aggressive city ways.

Black children, at the time of this writing, have become more aware of what they *might* be. Yet there still exists the caustic and continued stereotyping represented in the late Langston Hughes' penetrating observation that "Misery is when your white teacher tells the class that all Negroes can sing and you can't even carry a tune." (12) Black children confront our public schools and are not prepared for the culturally centralized demands that are immediately laid upon them. . . .

The Puerto Rican

Two decades ago, in the years after World War II, 90 percent of the people of the island of Puerto Rico were poor. In Oscar Lewis' study of Puerto Rican families, both on the island and in New York City, he defines the concept of a culture of poverty as more than being poor: Some who are poor in an economic sense do not live in a culture of poverty.

A culture of poverty, according to Lewis, also includes—along with those factors mentioned earlier—the key factors of lack of identification with a larger societal cause or history; a fatalism; a weak ego structure, especially among males; and a provinciality or lack of awareness of troubles or strife beyond one's own immediate confines. (16)

These traits have marked Puerto Ricans who, caught in the cycle of despair, much like the American black, heard about the great opportunities in the big cities on the mainland. Legislation of 1921 and 1924 stopped the flow of European immigrants to America, and the McCarran-Walter Act imposed a quota on British West Indian blacks. Southern black migration helped for a while to fill the need for low-skilled labor, but the industrial buildup for World War II created a demand that outstripped the supply. Puerto Ricans were American citizens to whom immigration laws did not apply, and so powerful incentives were set in motion to entice them from the island.

A compounding factor was Puerto Rico's distressing overpopulation, which saw more than a doubling of the population in half a century. (In 1900 the population per square mile in Puerto Rico was 280; by 1940 it was 546, and by 1950 it was 645.) There were always surplus laborers, a scarcity of goods, and an intolerably poor means of distributing the necessities.

The "Jíbaro" (a man of the soil), unable to sustain himself or his family, moved first to the largest cities of San Juan, Mayaguez, and Ponce, and then to the awesome, but still hopeful, mainland.

Puerto Ricans brought their hopes with them, and yet their despair. They were eager to work but lacked urban skills; they wanted to be American but spoke Spanish and still followed homeland customs. For most, there was disappointment and misery.

Arriving after the blacks, they discovered housing was already difficult to find. Their people included white-skinned, blue-eyed members and dark-skinned blacks, which was insignificant back on the island. Suddenly the lighter-skinned Puerto Ricans found it to their advantage to disassociate themselves from the blacks, while the latter—held by common bonds of language and land—struggled to remain unified. To be a Puerto Rican (whether black or not) separated one from the "colored," who were lowest on the American totem pole. In fact, to be "white" was even better, and so those Puerto Ricans who could "pass" found the temptation overwhelming.

Moving from one poverty culture, where energies were already focused upon survival and maintenance, to another compounded by ethnic and racial prejudice cemented the despair and hopelessness of the Puerto Rican immigrant. In urban American schools, his children found a mysterious and linguistically alien indoctrination system thrust upon them. The American process of acculturation, as implemented by our public schools, could be perceived as little more than an oppressive and overpowering force. The humility of Puerto Rican families kept them from questioning or protesting. And so the entire process of education, of gaining some semblance of power over their life styles, of feeling proud and good about themselves, and of climbing up and out of the culture of poverty escaped the Puerto Rican.

But some progress has occurred, and some changes have taken place. As second generation *Borinqueños* (the Indian word for the island of Puerto Rico is *Borinquen*) stand tall and identify themselves without shame, a new era unfolds in Spanish Harlem. The Borinqueño speaks Spanish with pride; he is eager to teach his children the history of their people, the struggle of Campos the independence fighter, the names of José de Diego, Ramón Betances, Muñoz Rivera. In the schools, some teachers are using more Spanish, and others are trying to avoid the typical shaming of the children for speaking their island language.

Back in the homeland, birth control measures have seen population figures level off, and a new "prosperity" has hit the island (Puerto Rico's per capita income in 1969 was still lower than that of Mississippi, the poorest state in the Union) so that over 20 percent of the people are no longer living in poverty. For the first time in decades, the flow of Puerto Ricans between New York and the island has turned about, and as the 1970s move on, more Puerto Ricans are actually leaving New York to return to Puerto Rico than vice versa.

The degradation that marked the urban, stateside Puerto Rican may be on the run. Groups of "do-it-ourselves" Borinqueños are infusing life and action into the slums of New York, and the effect could be uplifting to Puerto Ricans throughout the United States. The RGS (Real Great Society) is one such group, founded on Manhattan's Lower East Side in 1964. With pride, their spokesmen insist that they are ". . . the first organization in East Harlem which stresses and makes it blatantly clear that we are interested in Puerto Ricans and Puerto Ricanness." (11)

Interestingly, as Puerto Ricans begin to focus upon their own situation and to take action to alter it (Oscar Lewis has stated that when a people become organized and active in their destinies, as did those in the civil rights movement, the culture of poverty begins, by definition, to fade away), some workers in their ranks have come to the same conclusions that this present writing advances. "Power is what it is all about—power and pride," (11) says one writer. As stated by a leader in the RGS, "The people of this community must run this community. . . ." (11)

Puerto Ricans still have a long way to go in the urban centers of America. Part of the distance must be spanned by the dominant culture coming over to meet them. This is also true in education. Puerto Ricans in our schools must be allowed to remain Puerto

Ricans and still benefit from a sound education. Implementing this is the challenge that faces our teachers and our society.

The Mexican-American

Our discussion of the Mexican-American in an urban ghetto or *barrio* will be brief, because the conditions which exist for *Chicanos* * in America's Southwest cannot readily be separated into urban and rural clusters. Unlike the ghettoes or barrios of the East, the barrios of the West are most often characterized by single-family housing, some openness between houses, and a modicum of land or yard attached to each dwelling. It is still a barrio and it still represents poverty, but for the Chicano there is more of an element of actual rural physical living.

The Chicano who lives in a city must face one overpowering fact, however, that is not present on a ranchito or out on the countryside. His traditional way of living must come into constant contact and conflict with other cultural styles and beliefs. Though he is an American (the "original" American in much of the Southwest, since his ancestors on his Indian side go back hundreds of years before the coming of the *gabacho* [Anglo] to this land), he is still considered a "Mexican" by others in the larger culture.

The Chicano child in our schools must live with the constant sense of his difference, both in language and in life style. His parents are terrified by the pace and the sophistication of the educational system. Some would never think of complaining; others refuse to go to the school for meetings or conferences. Teachers are quick to note their "lack of cooperation" or "lack of interest" in their children's school progress.

Today, Chicano youth are also on the move. Mexican-Americans, much like blacks and Puerto Ricans, are culturally different, basically rural in their life styles, and have only been accepted into our dominant school system as they are willing to cast off aspects of their ancestry and culture. But there are signs that the schools are becoming aware of their past inflexibility. . . .

Black, brown, and some white Americans have been living in poverty in our country. Their life styles are unique to their particular ethnic and cultural heritages.

We propose here that the pervasive feeling of inadequacy among the poor stems much more from a lack of significant control over

---

* *Chicano* is the name taken by Mexican-Americans in the Southwest. Some older Mexican-Americans consider it a term of derision, but youths use it with pride.

their lives and destinies than from mere economic deprivation. Further, we hold that the life style of the poor is typically rural in origin and in manifestation and is currently incompatible with contemporary urban living. Let us next consider the characteristics of rural living.

---

1. Baldwin, James. *The Fire Next Time*. New York: Dial, 1963.

2. Baldwin, James. *Go Tell It on the Mountain*. New York: Dial, 1963.

3. Berne, Eric. *Games People Play*. New York: Grove, 1964.

4. Brookover, William B., and Thomas Shailer. "Self-Concept and School Achievement," *Sociology of Education*, 38, Spring 1964, p. 278.

5. Brown, Claude. *Manchild in the Promised Land*. New York: Macmillan, 1965.

6. Bruck, M. A. (doctoral dissertation), cited in: William W. Wattenberg, and Clare Clifford. "Relation of Self-Concepts to Beginning Achievements in Reading," *Child Development*, 35, June 1964, p. 461.

7. Carmichael, Stokely, and Charles V. Hamilton. *Black Power: The Politics of Liberation in America*. New York: Random, 1967.

8. Cleaver, Eldridge. *Soul on Ice*. New York: McGraw-Hill, 1968.

9. Dimitroff, Lillian. "Concept of Self and Teaching Culturally Different People," in *Children, Psychology and the Schools*, edited by Bryant Feather and Walter S. Olsen, Glenview, Ill.: Scott, Foresman, 1969, p. 91.

10. Ellison, Ralph. *Invisible Man*. New York: Random, 1952.

11. Genevieve, Ray. "The City," in *VISTA Volunteer*, 5, 9, September 1969, pp. 11, 12.

12. Hughes, Langston. *Black Misery*. New York: Paul S. Erickson, 1969. Reprinted by permission.

13. Lewis, Oscar. *Current*, December 1966, p. 28–32.

14. Lewis, Oscar. *A Study of Slum Culture: Backgrounds for La Vida*. New York, Random, 1968, pp. 3–21.

15. Maslow, Abraham. *Toward a Psychology of Being*. Princeton, N.J.: Van Nostrand, 1962.

16. Miller, Warren. *Cool World*. New York: Little, Brown, 1959.

17. Morse, William C. "Self-Concept in the School Setting," *Childhood Education*, 41, December 1964, p. 197.

18. Wattenberg, William W., and Clare Clifford. "Relation of Self-Concepts to Beginning Achievements in Reading," *Child Development*, 35, June 1964, pp. 465, 466.

19. Webster, Staten W., and Marie N. Kroger. "A Comparative Study of Selected Perceptions and Feelings of Negro Adolescents with and without White Friends in Integrated Urban High Schools," *The Journal of Negro Education*, 35, Winter 1966, pp. 55–61.

Notes

Chapter Two

Rural Life Patterns

They Harvest Despair

The adventure of arriving at a new place overwhelmed Virginia Lee. . . .

There was one question she wanted to ask, but she didn't dare. It formed on her lips, then faded, inarticulated: Where was the school that momma said might be here?

The truth was that the child knew the answer. She had seen enough of the camp; she realized its remoteness; she knew it was abandoned, deserted. It would be the same as the last place, and the one before that. There was to be no school.

Recent literature concerned with people who live in poverty has pointed out that there are two distinct classes of immigrants. One consists of the "classical" immigrants, who came to America from their native lands attempting to better their condition, and the other of in-migrants who exchange their rural American life styles for an urban setting. (7) The former were often welcomed in the spirit of cultural pluralism that seemed to be giving the American dream its strength and versatility. The latter are tolerated in the sullen acceptance of democracy as the guiding principle of the culture, yet socially rejected as an undesirable and somehow humiliating throwback. This cultural deviant, though admittedly American, has no single skin color, no specific ethnic origin, no geographical spawning ground—other than the rural vastlands of our country. . . .

To know that the urban ghetto dweller of today comes from a rural cultural pattern of living is not enough; one must also know and understand *what it is like* where he comes from. Why are so many in-migrating to urban areas and becoming members of the corps of urban poor?

Who Are the Rural Poor?

A distinction must be made between people who merely live away from the city and people who comprise the group we have called the rural poor. There are ranchers, farmers, cattlemen, oilmen, foresters, entrepreneurs, and others in the smaller towns who do not fit the category of rural poor. Our definition encompasses some who are employed by the above groups of people, some who are self-employed, and others who are largely unemployed.

While not making up a large portion of the total rural population, the American Indian has the largest proportion of its ethnic group living away from urban centers. Curiously, this too is beginning to shift. Mexican-Americans also have in the past lived in rural settings, but with the change in laws by Congress, banning the great influx of Mexican nationals (*braceros*) to harvest the crops (many stayed on illegally and lived in abject poverty), and with the mechanization of harvesting throughout the Southwest, the worker finds a diminishing means of sustenance and is rapidly inmigrating to the large centers of population.

Poor whites still comprise the greatest number of rural people whose living is below standard. They live largely in the smaller communities of the South, and in the mountain regions of the middle East. Industries such as coal mining, with the depletion of the natural resource and the diminishing consumer demand, have dismissed large numbers of workers who have their "plot of earth" but no means of making a living while staying there. In some cases, a heritage of several generations of workers in one industry has been suddenly terminated, and the family structure is strained to accommodate the father's lack of earning power. Large amounts of federal compensatory funds have been infused into these areas in an attempt to retrain people whose skills are no longer useful.

Michael Harrington, in his classic study, *The Other America,* comments eloquently on the plight of the rural poor whose skills have become archaic. During the fifties alone, a million-and-a-half people left the Appalachians and added to what Harrington calls "colonies of poverty in the cities." (4) The pattern is repeated among farm workers of the East Coast, the South, and the Southwest where, at the end of the 1950s, nearly two million men, women, and children worked as migrant farmers. With the bracero curtailment, some 400,000 fewer workers were "on the move," and as sophisticated machinery and consolidated farms became more prevalent, the number needed for useful work diminished even more. The farm worker, receiving small compensation for his labor, and seeing his jobs disappear, joined in the mass slide into the city. Harrington paints a poignant image of the contrast between the glorified "old America of the fields" with the dignity of the hardworking farm hand, and today's residue of itinerant farm workers, housed in poverty, schooled in misery, and living in what he calls "the nation's shame." (4)

Black Americans, too, were spawned in the rural hinterlands of our country. They were nurtured in the most improbable of all environments—in servitude, either in physical fact or psychologically, to a more powerful and more self-assured member of *Homo sapiens.* That blacks have now become city-dwellers does not alter the undeniable residue of forces which shaped their outlook on life.

Puerto Ricans who now live in our Eastern, big-city barrios were children of the soil in their native island. To be sure, some lived in the squalor of large Puerto Rican cities for several years before escaping to the mainland centers. But their basic life style remained rural, and they brought that style into urban America, where they chafed and erupted against the power of the dominant culture.

What is the nature of these rural cultures that we find in our center-city schools? How can our schools understand and encompass them in their curricula and teaching methods? What should we, in turn, expect from children of diversity?

About 600,000 Indians live in the United States today. Of these, one in every five is a Navajo and lives, for the most part, upon a reservation in the Southwest, mostly in Arizona and New Mexico.

The American Indian

A common mistake is to consider all Indian tribes to be alike. It is true that there are many similarities among Indians of all tribes, including the common heritage of land, battle, and subservience. But the differences are so great that to understand well what motivates a given group, one would need to study in depth its particular history, mores, theology, character, and general philosophy.

The excellent film *The Exiles* * portrays the identity crisis of today's Indian in the Southwest of our country. Is it right to remain Indian, to live the Indian life, to resist assimilation—or should one become a part of the great rush, to strive and achieve in middle-class America? The film shows those Navajos who leave the tribe to make it on their own in Los Angeles and ultimately become part of the great army of urban minorities who cannot get steady work and who are poorly equipped to fight the battle of the industrial-acquisitive society. They therefore take on the characteristics of their new sociological classifications: the ghetto-dweller, the urban poor, the disadvantaged. Thus, the question asked earlier is merely a rhetorical one for the Indian. He does not have a choice. He is what he is: the amber-skinned citizen with a heritage of outdoor, rustic, non-competitive living, poorly equipped to cope with the big city, poorly educated (largely unmotivated to learn in most school settings), yet titillated enough by the glamour of brash, electronic America, aware enough of himself and of others to know what he is *not,* and eager to escape the shame that the larger world has told him goes with his earthy life style.

The Indian has been made aware that his forefathers' style of living falls under the rubric "poverty"—that it is unwholesome, unclean, barbaric, and even communistic (for after all, the Hopi Indians reject competition and embrace lives of sharing). Many voices call to the Indian to modernize and urbanize—but he is enmeshed in his heritage, unprepared for the American way, and cannot seek his fortune in the jeweled city. His own identity is cast into crisis.

The major contact the Indian has with outside America is through encounters with the federal government (and, of course, with the tourist, who takes great pride in bargaining down the price of a basket or a rug—which the Indian overpriced in the first place knowing about the Anglo's pride!). The Bureau of Indian Affairs has a vast network of schools which try to do for the rural Indian what the inner-city schools try to do for Negroes or Mexican-Americans. The Indian sees the government as the enemy. He resents big government

* *The Exiles*, Contemporary Films, San Francisco

much as the worker of the 1920s and 1930s resented big management. The Indian today wants to organize (much as the workers did in forming their labor unions), to form amalgams of tribal councils into district and regional groups to gain power and to get some say over his life, largely to combat the stewardship of federal government.

Interestingly, the emerging, partly urbanized American Indian (generally speaking—which may be a danger) is not at all liberal in the political-economic sense. He is much too eager for freedom and personal identity to think of democracy. He is much like the early laissez-faire pioneer who made his own way in the world. The Indian, too, needs to feel that he can make his own way—he has never been permitted to try, and is now beginning to demand the right to do so. It is understandable that he feels no need to work for the so-called good of a society which has ignored *his* welfare, and that he refuses to relinquish his demands or be regulated. . . . The analogy that the emerging countries in Africa are fiercely nationalistic and not at all oriented toward the United Nations seems appropriate here.

Unlike other minorities, the Indian has not experienced much exploitation by big business. He has been largely sheltered by the United States Department of the Interior. Thus the "great white father" is the object of his resentment, and he sees all evil as emanating from Washington. And yet, some of the Indian leaders are quite aware that hasty or ill-conceived plans for assimilation would make the rural Indian but another urban poverty statistic. And so the Indian fights against the Omnibus Bill (a Paiute spokesman once told me that his people called it the Ominous Bill), a government plan to give private ownership of reservation land to the Indian. As might be expected, many of the younger, more energetic and militant leaders *want* the private ownership, while the older tribesmen resist it. The resistance is based on the information that where Indians had in the past been given ownership, they were unable to maintain their property, could not pay the taxes, and found their land and homes repossessed; thus they lost the one protection they had always been assured of: shelter. Many then drifted to the city areas and became costly additions to the welfare rolls.

The older tribesmen and some others insist that the answer cannot be assimilation until there is at least education. But the traditional educational incentives—success, money, and fame—seem not to tempt our Indian children. Many teachers have complained in bewilderment that "they seem to be just fine until they reach about the fifth or sixth grade and then they get a chip on their shoulders and won't learn a thing—what happens to them?" The fifth and sixth grades (ages 10–11) of course, mark the time of emerging self-awareness, of identification. The Indian child is not as "cute" as he was at six or seven, and commensurately less "adorable" to his white teachers, principal, counselor, etc. The world of reality begins to come into focus. Racism spreads its ubiquitous web, and the brown child is suddenly and forever aware of his difference.

The larger issue is that the difference has a very negative connotation. The child is not only different—he is badly different. He is not purposely degraded by his teachers, but is conditioned to value only the larger American culture, the world of competitive success, the fast worker, the obedient child. Thus family teachings and reverence for what John Collier, former United States Commissioner of Indian Affairs, has called, "the earth and its web of life," are made to seem foreign, unworthy, shameful. The identity crisis begins. . . .

In his book *Indians of the Americas,* (1) John Collier expresses in one sense resignation to both the slow erosion of the civilized world and to a total neglect for the meaning implicit in our Indian society; and in another sense is uplifted with hope for the future through a promulgation of the Indian way to all cultures. Collier feels that most Indian groups have been able to retain a rather remarkable reverence for human personality, for the natural resources of the earth, and for the intrinsic good of their society, despite enormous attempts for centuries to dehumanize them. He also predicts that the Indian way will ultimately rise in importance; that Indians will keep their cooperative forms of democracy (indeed may even embody a world movement), not only political but social and economic as well; and that nations will, in time, turn to the Indians for the secrets of beauty, wisdom, strength, community life, local democracy, and a oneness with the earth that could save the world from its rush toward mechanistic annihilation. (2)

But today, the pressure is on the Indian to conform and to "get with it." One typical example might serve to illustrate the point. In the Owens Valley, on the east slope of the Sierra Nevada Mountains in California and on into Nevada, the Shoshone and Paiute Indians live in and around small, semiresort towns. There is no industry in the area, and the Los Angeles Department of Water and Power owns a good share of the land (Los Angeles gets a major portion of its water supply from the Owens River), and has vested interest in keeping agriculture at a minimal, noncommercial level. As a result, the reservation Indians have no meaningful work and no means of earning money. Many are habitually idle, some fit the caricature of the drunken Indian, others retreat into themselves in confusion and shame. Given their surroundings and the pressure of the white man's culture, their historic way of life is impossible—yet they are effectively prevented from engaging in that culture in any productive way. To compound the situation, the Indian's wife can earn some money by working seasonally as a maid in the several motels. The wife then becomes the breadwinner (a remarkable parallel is to be seen here between this condition and the urban Negro situation where the male is too often emasculated by unemployment and degradation) and the force to be consulted in the home. Decisions tend to be made by the stable, working, emotionally sound woman, while the male loses his sense of importance, of dignity, and ultimately, of identity. The community smiles up its sleeve at the lazy, drunken Indians, and rises up in anger and self-righteousness when a crime is committed by "those damned wards of the state who just keep costing us money and won't do a lick of work. . . ."

Sadly and ironically, the end result of this unfortunate situation is that the Indian migrates to the city, taking with him his pastoral mode of life, his naiveté in urban competition, and his personal and emotional inadequacies. He thus increases the cost to the citizenry by receiving welfare and unemployment payments. And this adds to our national shame through the general decay of the inner city, festering and smoldering. Small wonder that Indian children come to the inner city school having little in common with the richly stimulated Anglo child—and even less in common with their college educated, often liberal but highly propagandized middle-class teacher.

Collier's hope for the spread of the Indian way refers to the uncontaminated Indian way; not the conditioned, coerced, corrupted way of the semiurbanized, partially competitive, laissez-faire Indian who now exists in the margins of the larger culture. The latter is the convert —and a tribute to our culture's inhumanity. The former remains, as Collier has said, as a beacon to "the long hope" that the world may again regain its reverence for human personality and its natural union with earth.

The Mexican-American

In the great, fertile San Joaquin Valley of California, where grapes, melons, cotton, citrus, and many other fruits, vegetables, and plants burst forth in tribute to the richness of the land, one of the remarkable paradoxes of earth exist. The harvest is one of the most abundant of all farmlands of the country, while its harvesters waste and languish from hunger and disease.

A class of mine, in fact, recently viewed eight children living in a two-room shack with their parents. The oldest two, in their early teens, picked grapes in the fields along with their mother and father from before dawn to sunset. The other five were supervised by the eldest remaining at home, a ten-year-old. One baby slept cross-wise on a cot with flies settled on his lips, cheeks, and eyelids. His even younger infant brother slept fitfully on another cot, his head burning with fever. Two ceramic pots were pushed under one cot; one, half filled with dried beans, was swarming with flies, while the other, a pot of moist beans, was protected by just a sheet of waxed paper. The children were delighted to show visitors through their house. They spoke some English, having gone to school in New Mexico. They would return to New Mexico in the winter to live and work in the lettuce fields in the early spring. The family followed the crops. When the grapes were done, the melons would be ready. If the week was good and all four workers worked, the yield was deceptively good: sometimes $200 for the week. But then the waiting and following and traveling and waiting. And sometimes no work for three weeks . . . And then—the coming of the machine.

Itinerant farm workers in California are from many areas and of many ethnic groups. Alongside the Mexicans work Filipinos, blacks, Puerto Ricans, some Anglos, and sprinklings of several other racial minorities. Until recently they had no unifying voice, and were literally at the mercy of the growers. Not only could the worker expect little security and virtually no continuity, but his children's school (which they would probably attend for no more than a few weeks) had very little relevance to their mode of living or their real needs. Imagine the incongruity of teaching a farm laborer's child for five hours a day about Sally running or John jumping, or even the historical significance of the California missions! Most of these children, some possibly descendants of the settlers of those missions, have never had a fair share of the civilization that those early settlings portended, and probably never will.

Today, some progress has been made, but not through government aid nor through the benevolence of the employer. Occasionally a leader appears who is unafraid, dedicated, touched with fire, and able to unite and stir his people. Cesar Chavez, a poor, diminutive, intelligent, deeply dedicated Mexican-American farm worker seems to be such a leader. His farm worker union has had unbelievably rough going, with not only the growers conspiring against him, but the older, more established unions, eager to get at the untouched mass of workers, competing for representation. But the United Farm Workers Organizing Committee, Chavez's group, has continued to grow and to struggle toward organizing perhaps the poorest and most undereducated group of working people in our country. They have done so with the periodic help of urban political and civil rights leaders who have engaged themselves in the fight. Boycotts continued against selected growers until mid-1970, and contributions aided workers excluded because of imported, "scab" labor.

I visited a vineyard in central California where some of the workers (mostly at another location in the same chain of farms) had gone on strike. Those still working spoke freely during the lunch break, as they ambled in from the fields to the wooden benches in the eating area. One Mexican woman told how she had been working for the same boss for 23 years and how she really had it pretty good because she didn't ". . . have to ask to go to the bathroom; if you gotta go, you just take off." She was quite proud that ". . . no one looks over your shoulder when you work; they let you alone." Then she concluded on a philosophical note that illustrated an irony she scarcely recognized, when she said, "We got it pretty good. We got nothing to complain. We gotta work. We were born poor."

Born poor! How that pervaded her entire outlook on life, her expectations, her demands, her belief in herself. It was later made known that while several of the women were long-time employees (a small cadre of pickers and hands are needed year-round as the owner directs his farm from the harvesting of one crop into the next), the vast majority of workers are only needed at "ripe" season, or the peak of the grape harvest. Of these itinerants, most had at that time gone on strike for better wages. When Chavez helped them to articulate their demands (which included $1.40 per hour minimum wage), the owners laid them off, rounded up busloads of farm hands from New Mexico, Oklahoma, and points south (one man and his 20-year-old son were from Mississippi), where the wages were generally 80¢ and 90¢ an hour, and promised to pay them $1.40 an hour! Thus the wage demands were being paid to imported workers, and the owners avoided bargaining with an agent they considered improper.

This struggle for better working conditions and salaries sets the stage for the situation that currently exists with the Mexican-American who has followed the crops. The mechanization of the farms has been slow—probably because of the abundance of cheap labor and the costly capital outlay of machinery. But with the awakening of the farm laborer and his demand for decent reward, the growers' reaction has been swift. Many are now beginning the conversion (for selected crops) to machines. The worker, much like the coal miner in the Appalachians, finds his skills archaic and unwanted.

Poorly schooled, having lived in transiency, handicapped by his bicultural conditioning, and penalized for his bilingualism, the Mexican-American picks his way toward the *barrios* of the city. There he may not find work, but he will find a common language, a similar heritage, and people who will accept if not exalt him. His children appear one day in our inner-city schools. They are shy, almost withdrawn, frightened, bewildered, hostile. The school at once classifies them (usually as "nonverbal") and writes them off from any meaningful stimulation.

Our major means of uniformly identifying children remains the intelligence test. We continue to place children in special classes for the educable mentally retarded (EMR) or the educationally handicapped (EH), by comparing them to normative groups on such tests as the Stanford-Binet and the Wechsler Intelligence Scale for Children. These are probably considered our most valid intelligence tests. Yet the groups from which these tests were standardized, and therefore *the population for whom they are intended,* do not include children of culturally diverse backgrounds or bilingual speech patterns. In administering such tests to Mexican-American children, I have found them useless in predicting educational potential. Their major use is to measure knowledge of the American idiom and the American home's pattern of enrichment (educational toys, puzzles, games, etc.). And this we really could have gauged without administering the test.

But our schools continue to make assumptions about the Mexican-American child based upon these culturally biased instruments. The child is often relegated to a special class and frequently offered a sterilized curriculum geared to what school officials believe to be his capability. One high school principal once made the point to a group of his teachers that "our children just can't achieve very well with intellectual-type offerings, so we emphasize vocational trades for them." The lack of challenge for the Mexican-American child becomes the mode, and his academic antipathy a self-fulfilling expectation.

To repeat—it must be pointed out here that the Mexican-American child from the rural background arrives in the center city with a self-image and a psychological make-up that poorly outfits him for the demands of the urban school. We have already commented on (and shall embellish on later in this writing) the irrelevancy of those demands and the need for the schools to take harder looks at their own positions and curricula. But our refrain here is really that the rural child carries with him an image of personal inadequacy, and that he is alienated, before he starts, from the strange and meaningless requests of the teacher and his school. How much more powerful the psychological degradation than the economic and the cultural!

In the hope of uncovering some general evidence about the educational retardation that the American migrant worker's children experience we shall turn briefly to some national findings. One recent research article proposes an economic hypothesis. (3) While wages are significantly lower for agricultural jobs than for urban jobs, few opportunities exist in the city for supplementing the income of a family whose breadwinner is unskilled and is the only worker. The worker, as his family grows, begins to search for ways to employ more members of the family. He turns to the farms.

A United States Department of Agriculture survey in 1964 found that 21 percent of migratory agricultural workers who worked as farm wage laborers for 25 days or more were 14–17 years of age. (8) By employing his children, the worker can supplement his income significantly, especially during peak harvest time. Conversely, when enough members of the famly can find stationary employment so that migrating becomes economically unnecessary, families tend to leave the farm-labor force. (6)

The hypothesis which seems to present itself is that children thus exploited economically suffer from marked educational retardation. It also appears that parents who thus "choose" for their children an economic path rather than an educational one are reflecting the attitude that since they have had little education themselves, only minimal education is really needed.

This has implications for the social involvement of the parents in the schools, the value placed upon achieving by their children, and the amount of discussion about school and related educational matters in the home. Little wonder that the child from such a background has the highest adolescent school drop-out rate of any group!

Partly to blame for this condition is the "agribusiness" itself, which permits and encourages child labor. The laws which protect children from industrial exploitation have little effect on agricultural institutions. This is not to say that the laws do not exist. The Fair Labor Standards Act regulates employment of children in agriculture under 16 years of age if the products go into interstate or foreign commerce. Such children are not to be employed during school hours. But the Act is inadequately funded, and therefore it goes largely unenforced. Our farm workers' children must face the choice of moving at once from childhood to the self-disciplining wage-earner's role, or of moving through a guidance phase in which the experiences in an educational environment attract their loyalties.

The latter choice has not prevailed. The migrant child is proud of his "picking" ability, and ashamed of his academic ineptitude. It is natural that he eases away from our educational system.

Other Mexican-Americans

But there are Mexican-Americans who have rural environmental histories, who live in the depths of our cities, and who have never worked as farm laborers in this country. These are the immigrants, the wet-backs, the domestics, the relatives of United States citizens, the friends of long-time residents. Some have come here on visitors' visas and stayed; others have come on temporary work visas and stayed; still others are here legally through the efforts of relatives and friends. They come, largely, from the rural provinces in Mexico. They seek "a newer world" and a better chance for their children. They are relatively contented during their early years in America; the unrest comes when awareness begins. . . . But what are the characteristics of these rurally nurtured Mexican-Americans who live in our cities?

Of Roman Catholic faith and with minimal formal education, they appear to know little about methods of birth control of either the religiously acceptable or unacceptable kinds. Their families grow quickly, outdistancing the wage-earner's ability to support them. The mother, often coping with several young children and at the same time pregnant with yet another, enlists the aid of the oldest child for housework and baby care. This child, still of school age herself, finds the demands upon her critically divisive, and she most frequently chooses her family obligations at the expense of homework, school activities, and friendships. The effect upon her academic achievement is obvious. Less obvious, but still significant, is the effect upon her involvement in the larger culture. The young Mexican-American boy feels the pressure upon him to aid the family income as soon as he is strong enough to work, and so he too sacrifices educational achievement.

Mexican-American family studies show a great closeness and a strong filial tie that exclude a large part of the outside world. It is important to note the effects of (1) birth proliferation, and (2) economic inadequacy on this situation. While we make no judgment on desirability of close-knit families, loyalties such as exist among Mexican-American families in the inner cities of the Southwest do tend to preempt involvement in the Anglo culture. It is not surprising that feelings of inadequacy develop in children thus excluded, which grow and pervade their entire life style.

When one talks of Mexican-Americans not achieving, it is from the perspective of achievement based upon Anglo middle-class standards. Take, for example, a criterion of motherliness as concommitant with success, and it might be found that the Mexican-American woman is eminently successful; or take "machismo," which roughly translated is manliness, as a criterion for success, and we would find most Mexican-American men highly successful. To understand a culture, then, is to uncover the motivating forces in a peoples' life style.

It is also important to tie together the Mexican-American pattern of family cohesiveness with a historical precedent: In an alien situation, groups tend to band together for mutual need, nurture, and security. Immigrants of virtually every national background have followed this pattern in the United States, especially if a language difference has existed. (Of course, we might also be commenting here upon the negative attitude of the born American for the transplanted one.) The Anglo expects the person of Mexican ancestry to be something less than a hard worker. There are the lingering "siesta" and "mañana" Anglo generalizations. Stereotyped as these notions are, they tend to be self-fulfilling prophecies. What is expected of a person often conditions his behavior. One is reminded here of James Baldwin's comment that black maids in wealthy homes deliberately nip the liquor because they know the white boss will expect them to.

But again, the pervading issue haunts us: *Should* Mexican-Americans take on the characteristics of the middle-class American culture? Or is there opportunity for a life style that is diverse and totally unique to flourish alongside the mainstream one—and not just exist (to live in poverty and disease is to exist) but *flourish,* with ample food, lodging, clothing, relaxation, and comforts? We must once again ask whether we are able to tolerate cultural pluralism under this vast, tattered, unpredictable umbrella we call America. The implications of this question for our educational system deserve careful scrutiny. Has the major goal of our public schools been one of indoctrination rather than exploration, of conformity rather than uniqueness?

A final point to consider is the knotty problem of bilingualism. **Bilingualism** With no other culturally different group has a different primary language posed such difficulty as with the Spanish-speaking Mexican-American. An impartial observer would surely look upon a bilingual person as rather uniquely gifted, but most of us are so enmeshed in the "problem" that we think of it as a deficiency. That is, we expect our children of Mexican ancestry to have a language problem before we start with them. We view them (as early as in the preschool Headstart program) as nonverbal, while in reality they are quite verbal, quite communicative, but in a different verbal style than we might expect. It has often been quite astonishing to visit a school where a teacher has complained about the verbal inadequacies of her very young children, and to hear how garrulous such children are when talking to each other!

One hypothesis which might explain why being bilingual creates a problem for Mexican-American youth is the fact that we are close to Mexico. No other ethnic group in America could travel by land to their homeland and to the total involvement with their former language and culture so easily as the Mexican-American. A youngster in the American barrio is conditioned in Spanish (to think, to talk, to reason) from the cradle on, is influenced by the street and the neighborhood to understand some English, and then is thrust into the school setting where only English is demanded. He returns to his home each day and is reinforced in Spanish. The barrio in the big city (Los Angeles, Phoenix, Albuquerque) is large and virtually self-sufficient. The native language, then, in behaviorist terms, is operantly conditioned to be retained and to be used. Not alert to this bond that is being reinforced, the school exhorts, cajoles, indeed punishes children to make them "say it in English."

The language issue is indeed tragic. One Spanish-speaking domestic worker up from a small town in central Mexico recently told me (in Spanish) how she could not understand why all the Mexican-American young people she met in a church group in Los Angeles had "verguenza" (shame) about speaking Spanish. She had joined the club because the priest had advertised it as a Spanish-speaking group. But when they met, the boys and girls (ages 16–22) voted to conduct all meetings in English.

But there is hope and there is progress. In California, a recent legislative action is permitting some primary school classes throughout the state to be taught in Spanish. The hypothesis which supports and which influenced this action suggested that the conversion to learning in English is possible and even enhanced when a Spanish-speaking child has a rich and stimulating start in his own tongue. Indeed, I have had personal experience to support such a thesis; in counseling with and testing youngsters who had in-migrated from urban areas in Latin America, I found that among those educated in Spanish who were now bilingual and living in America, no poverty of ability, of verbal capacity, or of intelligence could be found.

What we have said is that the bilingualism is not, of itself, a handicap. It is the lack of enrichment, of stimulation, of exposure; in a word, it is the *rural* influence that handicaps our youth when asked to perform basically urban tasks in our schools. And our schools have been structured to demand only the urban-influenced learnings; until recently, no attempts had been made to refocus the *school's* energies and expectations.

The Puerto Rican   Youngsters of Puerto Rican ancestry in our Eastern, big-city barrios are also bilingual, and what has preceded applies in part to them. But Puerto Ricans have a unique rural legacy. They are aliens to the mainland and live with an inexorable sense of their "foreignness"; Mexican-Americans were inhabitants of the Southwest earlier than the Anglo, and they are beginning (especially the youth) to promulgate a sense of their identification and belonging to the land. But both groups have had their native, rural cultures rejected by the dominant culture and thus face the sense of their difference in the cities and in the schools.

The Puerto Rican who is transplanted to the continent grows up having to deal with a process of identification. He is more urbanized than his parents, has two languages, is bicultural, is neither white nor black. The rural, island part of his culture has for a long time been influenced by the Spanish and by the American cultures. It has been minimally influenced by the indigenous (Arawak) Indian culture of the island and so has less of the folk arts or aboriginal customs than some other Latin American countries. In contrast to other West Indian countries, Puerto Rico's slave population retained very little of its Afro cultural origins. At the same time, in Puerto Rico the Indians were largely absorbed or killed off very early. The Spanish influence remained and dominated until 1898, when the first North American troops landed in Puerto Rico in the Spanish-American War. From then on, the primary culture of the island became a blend of American and Spanish.

The primary religion of the island has always been Catholicism. But since the advent of United States sovereignty, Protestant sects have been growing. Some 15 percent of the population had shifted to some form of Protestantism (usually Evangelical, Seventh-Day Adventist, or Pentacostal) by the end of the 1960s. But the strong hand of the Catholic church shaped the value system and behavior patterns of the population, and continues to be a primary force in its stress upon the dominant family structure and the prime place of the father.

Spiritualism and witchcraft are prevalent in Puerto Rico and tend to supplement the formal Christian liturgies. Contrary to hearsay, anthropologists have reported no significant relationship between witchcraft and the heavily African-influenced areas of population. In fact, some evidence indicates less influence of black magic in the all-black areas than in other communities.

The Puerto Rican family is mainly patriarchal and authoritarian; the male is the leader and commands respect and obedience. However, many marriages are common-law (some estimates run as high as one-quarter), and so, many births occur out of wedlock (as many as one-third). Still, Puerto Rican custom is that the man assumes responsibility for all his children, whether born of one mother or more. The law in Puerto Rico requires that the names of both parents be recorded on the birth certificate, whether married or not, and the child born out of wedlock is permitted to use the father's family name.

Puerto Rican families have a custom of relative freedom for young males, but extreme overprotection of young females. The father tenaciously guards the virginity of his daughters, and often displays hostility to would-be suitors. Courtship, then, is carried on through an intermediary, and marriage occurs through an escape or an elopement. The young girl is expected to be married by 18 or 19, and marriage is not uncommon at the age of 13 or 14 among the more rural peoples of the island. Early childbearing is the rule rather than the exception, and a strong institution of godparents (*compadres*) offers second parents in case of family problems.

Coming to America casts the traditions and the habits of the island culture into immediate and constant crisis. Coming into our schools creates relationship problems that neither the schools nor the families are prepared to understand. On the island, the school is a second home—the teacher a second mother. It is not uncommon for a family to send a sick child to school expecting the school to care for him. The school must nurture the child and also discipline him; right of corporal punishment is granted as readily as right of love and affection. A child will often hide his head rather than face a confrontation with an authority figure. Children will not look into the face of an adult when speaking with him. The home teaches absolute respect for authority and expects no back talk. The schools in Puerto Rico expect the same. . . .

In America, where the child has been urbanized but his parents have not, a crisis exists. Father is still the parent to deal with when the school must consult the family, even though he takes no active responsibility in rearing the child and may even need an interpreter to speak for him. Often, the father's role is cast into crisis by the child's being so much more sophisticated than he. Often, the father is humiliated by his inability to provide for his family on the mainland while his wife (especially in New York and Chicago) can get work in the needlework or other women's trades. Often, the mother throws up her hands in desperation at her attempt to discipline her children with old standards in a new setting. The overall picture is confusing, painful, and—as yet—unresolved. It is a vivid example of culture clash and the agony of the inability to understand or cope with it.

The Puerto Rican child in an urban, mainland center is a complex amalgamation of several cultures back on his island homeland plus the subculture around him in his new mainland home. There are extreme conflicts between parent and child and between the children of Puerto Rican ancestry and children of other American groups. Some of the conflicts result in parental reaction which is very severe and restrictive (further confusing the child who is trapped between his several worlds), or in resignation and desperate referral to social agencies which presumably are skilled in helping children gone bad.

The schools are not prepared to comprehend the cultural complexities which bombard the Puerto Rican child in America. Language programs are tried and have varying success. Programs to involve the parents are tried, but have minimal influence.

Today, many Puerto Ricans are going back to the island to regain equanimity in their life styles. But doubt remains, because poverty and overpopulation and lack of opportunity also remain back on the island. As late as 1969, the misapprehensions about the urban paradises on America's mainland still beckoned and enticed and misled. A popular song in the fall of 1969 seemed to have caught, rather incisively, the flavor of the "impossible dream" that continued to proselyte the poor and the different: "I Guess the Lord Must Be in New York City." A sequel might say: "Where Has He Gone now That We're Here?"

The Black

Let us accept that black Americans come from a rural people, because of their former condition as slaves and the half century of unequal, rustic, precarious freedom which followed; and that the last 50 years of migration into and encapsulation within urban areas has done little to alter their basically rural life mode. The black man who lives in the city has been denied access to the majority culture; he has, in effect, been rejected, kept from assimilating, ghettoized. And the pervasive effects of poverty have further complicated his life style.

His rural background comes from his homeland too, though it gets lost in his centuries of servitude. What needs to be understood, however, is that black Americans were as influential in shaping the culture of the American South as were their white masters. Students of language have duly noted that the so-called Southern drawl is very likely a product of the mixture between English and the native African dialects imported along with the slaves. Black Americans, then, do not speak a Southern white dialect; it is as correct to say that white Southerners speak a black dialect. . . .

Black Americans are relatively recent urban dwellers. In 1790, 91 percent of all Negroes lived somewhere in the South. The first large migration to the cities came during World War I, when labor was needed to fight the war and when agricultural needs were being changed by the delayed onset of the industrial revolution in the South. In 1910, 73 percent of all Negroes lived in rural areas; by 1960, 73 percent lived in urban areas (a larger percentage than the urban white population). (5)

Blacks from the rural South were, in the words of the more militant leaders of today's movements, "niggerized" by their white masters. Their familial relationships under slavery were totally destroyed (except where Catholic slave traders operated, along the New Orleans–Mississippi delta area) and men were used as studs for breeding. Blacks were kept so animalized that even little children were separated from their mothers when old enough to work and care for themselves. The defenses that were developed were inextricably woven into the fabric of their slave condition.

The music that grew out of slavery pleaded for freedom: "All God's chillun got shoes; when I get to hebbin I'm gonna get me some shoes." (Where was heaven? North, across the Ohio River!) "Jordan River is chilly and cold, hallelujah, chills the body but not the soul, hallelujah." (What river is the Jordan? The Ohio!) And when the masters heard their darkies singing about heaven, they scoffed, "What do we care if they want to go to heaven. Let 'em go." And many did go: "One of these nights 'bout two o'clock, this old world's gonna reel and rock; Pharaoh's army got drownded, oh Mary don't you weep."

Much later, after the Civil War and on into the 1880s when some semblance of family structure began to pertain to black people, the blues developed. The patterns of living that dominated the slave condition were not easily discarded, and so the woman was forced to cry out to the world over and over again, "My man done left me; I got the blues 'cause my man done up and left me." Today's so-called urban Negro's family crises are indeed deeply saturated by the effects of the Negro's former slave existence. . . .

Some observers of America's rural slave society have drawn distinctions between those blacks who were house servants and those who worked in the fields ("house niggers and field niggers"). Those who were house servants were the favored, the lighter-skinned, the more likely to be given some education. There was much copulation between the master and the female house slave, less between the master and the field slave. Offspring of the former were more likely to be favored. In the years just after emancipation, some of the more favored were sent away to the North to get some schooling (a matter of pride with the white father and master, yet a face-saving device). Often they stayed, but sometimes they returned with tales of the great opportunities for black people. The rumors began, and great yarns were spun about liberty and equality and luxury. America's cities of the North were beckoning, but the black people from the South had few of the skills needed for survival in the highly structured urban centers. They came and were lost.

They came with their farm backgrounds, their rustic educations, their slave psychologies, their unschooled dialects. They came with their loose family structures, their emasculated men, their overwhelming sense of their own inadequacies. The field blacks had more compelling and apparent reasons to leave, and so the flow to the North was largely composed of the least educated and least prepared of the blacks. They came with hopes and with naivete, with ambition but without resources; and they were poor.

The cities reacted with predictable concern. Unable to prohibit the in-migration of the Southern black (indeed, needing the muscle in his arm), the white city folk managed to channel his off-work activities into specified geographic units. Jealous of their own urban culture and very frightened of the rural black culture, the whites effectively protected themselves by sealing off the black man's domestic and social access. "He can work for us, but we don't have to be exposed to him beyond that," was the message.

And blacks from the South, arriving with enthusiasm but trepidation, got the message. They examined themselves and found themselves lacking—and their sense of self-worth sank lower. The psyche of the urban-living, ghettoized, rurally nurtured black American began to take form.

But slavery and the oppression of the system had had other effects as well. Black people had to learn to rely on each other; they developed a kind of cooperative, sharing existence. They became to each other brothers. They became strong in endurance and in coping with adversity. The women became unusually self-sufficient and resourceful. Families were extended and mutually supportive. Grandparents and uncles and aunts became intrinsic parts of the family. A kind of rustic intuition was carefully nurtured (more on this will be discussed in a later chapter), born out of having to react to the moods of the white man and not only to his words.

The rural black man had come to the city to seek his fortune. Public schools were waiting for him. But they did not understand him—nor he them. His already deflated sense of self became overwhelmed by the bewildering routine and demands of the schools and their teachers. He could not see the relevance of their curriculum; they could not see his abilities. Conflict, chaos, low test results, poor grades, dropouts, minimal scholarship, few entrants into college—the Negro in America has reaped the harvest of despair that the seeds of his rural culture have sown.

There are other Americans, too, who are different, poor, and powerless. There are white poor and Oriental poor, and there are the poor who have refused to cast off their old-world religions or customs. All of these poor have had one unifying trait: they have been culturally different from middle-class America's life style. Each also has its unique traits, which deserve some attention. But we shall not

attempt to describe the rural backgrounds or the present urban conditions of each of these subgroups at this point. It is not their specific
differences, but the mere fact that they are different which makes them
undergroups in our society. That is our thesis. For now, we must move
to an examination of the generalized problems confronting those who
are different and poor who face our educational network. For now,
we must seek an understanding of the motivations of those who are
poor, and the characteristics of the school system which they confront.

Notes

1. Collier, John. *Indians of the Americas.* New York: Mentor Books, 1947.

2. Collier, John. *Indians of the Americas.* New York: Mentor Books, 1947, pp. 186–187.

3. Fasick, Frank A. "Educational Retardation among Children of Migratory Workers," *Rural Sociology,* 32, 4, December 1967, pp. 399–413.

4. Harrington, Michael. *The Other America.* New York: Macmillan, 1962, pp. 45, 62.

5. Hauser, Philip M. "The Chaotic Society: Product of the Social Morphological Revolution," *American Sociological Review,* 34, 1, February 1969, pp. 7, 8.

6. Metzler, William H., and Sargent, Frederick O. "Incomes of Migratory Agricultural Workers," College Station: Texas Agricultural Experimental Station, Bulletin 950, March 1960, p. 7.

7. Ravitz, Mel. "The Role of the School in the Urban Setting," in A. Harry Passow, editor, *Education in Depressed Areas.* New York: Teacher's College, Columbia University, 1963, pp. 6–23.

8. *USDA, AER,* 82, Washington, D.C.: Government Printing Office, 1965, p. 11.

Chapter Three

Psychological Health of the Poor

Minstrel Man

Because my mouth
Is wide with laughter
And my throat
Is deep with song,
You do not think
I suffer after
I have held my pain
So long?

Because my mouth
Is wide with laughter
You do not hear
My inner cry?
Because my feet
Are gay with dancing
You do not know
I die?

Langston Hughes. From The Dream
Keeper, *by Langston Hughes. Copyright
1932 and renewed 1960 by Langston
Hughes. Reprinted by permission of
Alfred A. Knopf, Inc.*

Classic studies of behavior patterns of people who live in poverty emphasize the incidence of measurable neuroses or psychoses compared to the middle-class or upper-class populations. Statistical studies have implied greater psychoses among people in Class V (lower class) and greater neuroses among people in Classes I and II (upper classes). (4) Other researchers have challenged such findings by computing the data from different angles and with different statistical devices. (5) In short, there is not complete agreement about psychological health or its lack among people of poverty. One finds himself examining carefully the numerous definitions of "health." Rather than employing the standard definitions of mental illness or mental health, we shall consider the situation from a very practical, nonmedical viewpoint. We shall define mental (psychological) health to be: living with a minimum of personal and social disorder, functioning with some personal satisfaction, and containing a self-concept that is adequate and dynamic.

But phrased thusly, and without further clarification, it is also easy to see how people of poverty could be considered, in many instances, as generally rather less than psychologically healthy. The hypothesis could be presented that the psychological health of any subgroup, measured within, and compared to, a given culture, can be made to appear poor because of, *ipso facto,* the definitions of good and poor health: Those are healthy who are in harmony with the social order and those are not who are in disharmony.

This, however, can also be simplistic if not carefully analyzed. Our above definition of good health emphasizes the individual's personal (phenomenological) conceptualizing of himself as a human being of worth and value. While this certainly cannot be done independent of a social order, it can be done *despite* the values of a given social order. A person of poverty, then, feeling himself rejected by the larger culture could *still* be psychologically healthy by identifying his "self" and his behavior with other reference groups or subcultures. The angry and militant black nationalist groups, by these definitions, serve a valuable function in providing one segment of the society with a meaningful identification.

We are saying that the poverty-stricken individual, despite alienation from the culture at large, can be in a state of satisfactory equilibrium with himself through some felt relationship to a subsegment of the culture. But we must also ask how long the person can tolerate the rejection by the larger culture, and when and in what form he begins to manifest signs of alienation, disorder, and unhappiness within himself, and a subsequent failure to function in a progressive, fulfilling way. We also ask how many people of poverty do *indeed* have any kind of reference group with which they can identify and which can give them meaningful social involvement. This will not be discussed in a statistical sense, nor with psychiatric labels. Rather, we shall explore the functional equality of people in poverty as they are forced to react to and interact with the prejudices, controls, power, bureaucracies, politics, economics, and general whimsy of the American scene.

Most people who live in poverty just don't think very much of themselves. There are many confusing, complicated reasons for this, a significant one being the message they are constantly getting from the culture at large. It was noted earlier that mass communication offers opportunities for instant comparisons. People of poverty can see at a glance the accumulation of goods the larger culture enjoys; but even more significant, they can see and hear and feel the thematic pertinence of most of the shows and stories and games that television and theaters present. The irrelevance of much of this material to the lives of most of the ghetto viewers is instantly apparent. The pervasive domestic situation comedies, for example, are saying: "Here are the tricky and superficial problems that an affluent family spends its time confronting." And they are also saying: *"You* do not spend your time at these problems because you cannot gain the position that permits you to engage in such leisure-time tomfoolery."

The Feeling of Adequacy

But even more profound is the message that the bureaucratic structure pumps out with unending regularity; a message which is, indeed, becoming so complex that to be able to cope adequately, the standard requirement, even for middle-class citizens, has become a college degree. The bureaucracies confound, frustrate, humiliate, and degrade the poor. The poor are managed, manipulated, and chastised for not knowing, and criticized for not being industrious. They avoid the bureaucracy and are accused of law breaking. They confront it and are exploited. The result is a totally helpless feeling—a feeling of inadequacy.

I made a rather significant personal discovery a short while back, while working as a counseling psychologist in a college counseling center. In the course of a year, of some 60 student-clients who came for academic-personal counseling, virtually everyone seemed to have a "hang-up" on some sexual problem, either guilt feelings for too much sexual activity, or panic because of fear of the opposite sex. The evidence seemed to show that Freud was indeed correct: Sex is the basic human motivation.

But upon deeper reflection and a more critical case-analysis approach, it soon became clear that in *every* case, the young man or woman did not think very much of himself. He did not like himself very much, he could not cope well, he did not feel very adequate. This saturated all areas of his life, including the sexual, which at that age (18–25) is certainly at a high-energy point. I found that to approach these clients' problems as basically sexual did little to raise their level of personal confidence and ability to function dynamically. Approaching the problems as more general feelings of inadequacy opened the clients to a self-investigation that seemed, empirically, to direct them to fuller personal lives.

The hypothesis that emerges herein parallels much that is being said about the poor and the powerless. The feeling of inadequacy seems to saturate their lives and to restrict their functioning at high levels of personal achievement and satisfaction.

But *inadequate* is really another way of saying *powerless*. If we reason carefully it may be seen that when a person is feeling better about himself, he is feeling some control over a given area of his human activity. The more areas he feels adequate in, the more control he has over his performance—the more he has power.

Of course, with our college students, the opportunity to gain feelings of adequacy and to have power over their activities was interpersonal in nature and was available so long as the contaminating personal relationships could be confronted. With powerless people of poverty, the avenue to adequacy is less personally available; the relationship is more cultural-personal and less interpersonal. . . . Through its oppression and complexity, the culture imposes upon its poor a feeling of inadequacy, and the way to better functioning is impeded by the refusal of those who have power to relinquish it.

The psychological health of the poor, then, can be considered in relationship to their opportunity for meaningful control over their own lives. And if the larger culture denies them this, the poor must seek alternatives. One of these is to ignore the larger culture and commit themselves to their own, internally defined, internally rewarding subculture. A corollary is to reject and condemn that culture which has denied them access and personal enhancement: And so the "revolution of the urban poor."

But are the poor uniformly in poor psychological health? They can find adequacy and, therefore, some sense of power, by identification with and subsequent reward from groups and causes germane to the urban poverty condition. This can give the committed poor psychological health. But those poor who have no reference group, who have no basis for self-identification, who suffer from "anomie," who feel inadequate and powerless to confront the daily struggle, are indeed suffering from poor psychological health. (It must be re-emphasized here that the imputation of personal, genetic, hereditary, congenital, or ethnic inadequacy is totally rejected; our thesis holds that the urban slum dweller is psychologically inadequate in direct relationship to the environmental control he is experiencing.) The implications for educating the poor in our public schools that stem from this notion are enormous.

One excellent comparison between the generally accepted "truths" about the poor and an alternate thesis of personal power or its lack has been made by Haggstrom, (2) who has gathered a quantity of data from publications relating to poverty written by social scientists over a 15-year span. In general, these publications stress widely varying hypotheses in describing behavior patterns of the poor. A primary hypothesis has been that money is the key to successful participation in the American scene. That is, the major problem of the poor is their poverty. This supposes that because the psychological characteristics of poor people represent certain inadequacies in behavior and attitude, such characteristics are the *result of* being poor. The cause and effect thesis, according to Haggstrom, has not been successfully demonstrated. In fact, he cites several instances where economic poverty exists (certain religious groups, leaders of the poor, college students from poverty homes) and psychological inadequacy does not. The latter tend to be quite committed to personal fulfillment, to various causes which they have pursued and embraced, and to have some form of future-time allegiance.

Other observations have cited: (1) lack of future orientation of the poor; (2) hostility toward those who have made it; (3) suspicion and resentment of outside influence; (4) a consequent trusting to "chance," "luck," or "fate"; (5) an apathetic approach to problems; (6) a futility about where everything is going and what everything means; and (7) childlike dependency on those who are gifted or capable or affluent or powerful.

While these findings cannot be refuted, a critical point must be made—that none of the above is more than an observation about what exists. None of the above is explanatory, but rather largely descriptive. None of it gets at the heart of the matter.

Haggstrom explores these phenomena by citing the syndrome of psychological dependency and its concommitant loss of self-esteem. His notion of psychological dependency would appear to neatly parallel our earlier hypothesis about feelings of inadequacy. The dependent person has lost the capacity to make decisions and to rely upon his own abilities. Completing the circle, he then diminishes in his belief that he has any control over his own destiny, and he feels lost and helpless, inadequate, powerless. This description of the existential situation of the poor, when read with an understanding of the thesis of inadequacy or of powerlessness, becomes much more comprehensible.

The debilitating aspect of the dependency of the urban poor, in contrast with the dependency of other segments of our society (workers dependent upon their management, or children upon their parents), is their lack of opportunity to influence personally and actively a change in their situation. If the poor had access to the means for change or saw some slight opportunity for choice in their condition, the psychological impact of their situation would be lessened.

The Do-It-Your- self Thesis

But what might alter this helplessness of spirit that characterizes poor people? Middle-class Anglo citizens are becoming increasingly aware of their own historical neglect of the poor in their cities; but are they yet aware that it behooves *them* to see the situation drastically altered? The militant blacks in our ghettoes have been crying out to the world that the awakening has come, that self-awareness is now upon the black poor, and that this country will not survive if the power structure does not bend to the demands of reality. What then, can white middle-class America do? In short, how is it possible to raise the personal expectations of those who feel inadequate and to enhance their lives so that they feel emotionally and psychologically capable?

In society at large, the poor must personally and collectively take social action to influence their own condition. They must also be unquestionably aware that *they* are the source of such action. The poor must see themselves as able to influence their own lives and environments. Thus, psychologically, they will begin to develop a sense of their own personal power and adequacy. Also, such action must have the effect of being able to move existing social institutions. It must have the ring of success—failure in self-initiated activities is likely to be as damaging in the beginning as failure in middle-class activities has always been.

And so we say that the poor must do it for themselves. Not without help, certainly, and not without many false starts and mistakes. But the ultimate thrust cannot be applied from the outside. Good health is generated from the energy released during meaningful thought and action. But middle-class, white, established powerful America cannot sit on its hands and demand that the poor help themselves "as we did when we were working our way up." One cannot demand that people pull themselves up by their own bootstraps if the people have never had boots. The poor must be involved, activated, motivated—and the nonpoor must be economically and emotionally receptive, willing to give away segments of their power, tolerant of diversely paced and managed activities mingling with and affecting their own, eager to cut tape and bend rules to help others as well as themselves.

I recently witnessed a black college student verbally castigate an important college administrator because the administrator had deferred a significant question (concerning recruitment of black college students) for "committee action." The student literally used the language of the streets in exhorting the administrator to "break the rules to bring more black kids in here, because you sure break 'em fast enough when it's somethin' *you* want!" It is true that we all could think of incidents where we have "exercised our power" to get tickets to a play or ball game, or to get a more favorable number at registration, or whatever. We call it pulling strings; divorced of metaphor, it is simply expressing our control or power over our environment.

The black student was soundly criticized by other administrators and faculty for his "disgusting exhibition" and his "humiliating display." One young college administrator noted that the student was "psychotic, disturbed, paranoid," in the lack of control he displayed over his own emotions. I profoundly disagree.

We have argued that personal power to control one's environment brings a sense of identity and a more sound psychological encounter with living. If this is true, then the person who has escaped the lethargy of dependency, who has attached himself to a cause or an ideal, and who takes dynamic action to forward his cause, is illustrating emerging psychological stability. That this student was actively pursuing, with shrewd volatility, a personally identified critical goal, was evidence of his growing emotional health. That he used a language and a style of presentation that proved offensive to the power structure was evidence of their absorption with the delivery and not with the message. This is not to say that "dirty" language must become the vogue, but we must not let the style cloud the message.

Ironically, the campus administration responded to the confrontation by implementing (within a 48-hour period) several programs of tutoring and curriculum revision that would remarkably and positively affect incoming minority students. Red tape was left strewn all over the campus. . . .

Participants, Not Recipients

It is fitting that we should close this section by citing the writings of Charles V. Hamilton, who with Stokeley Carmichael wrote *Black Power: The Politics of Liberation in America.* (1) It was Carmichael who first frightened powerful, middle-class America with his demands for black power. Subsequently, in the light of emerging strategies and increasing positions of importance for black people (and also, for Mexican-Americans, Puerto Ricans, and others), the rationale behind Carmichael's demands has become more comprehensible, less shocking to the general society.

Hamilton, in an article in the *New York Times Magazine,* (3) has written that the aim of black power is to "reduce black dependence upon whites." He also writes that black power seeks to ". . . work to establish legitimate new institutions that make participants, not recipients, out of a people traditionally excluded from the fundamentally racist processes of this country." Gauged within the framework of our hypothesis, such writing appears indeed wise.

How many of our people of poverty do identify with a cause, do feel personal strength, and meaningful social involvement? Our guess is, not many. Certainly not enough. But the tide is moving. *Power* becomes a rallying cry, and power is the key to dynamic living.

And so, we come to our schools. What kind of education can offer sound psychological health through meaningful involvement and a relevant curriculum?

Notes   1. Carmichael, Stokely, and Charles V. Hamilton. *Black Power: The Politics of Liberation in America.* New York: Random, 1967.

2. Haggstrom, Warren C. "The Power of the Poor," in Frank Reissman, Jerome Cohen, and Arthur Pearl, editors, *Mental Health of the Poor.* New York: Free Press, 1964, pp. 205–223.

3. Hamilton, Charles V. "An Advocate of Black Power Defines It," *New York Times Magazine,* April 14, 1968.

4. Hollingshead, August B., and Frederick C. Redlick. *Social Class and Mental Illness.* New York: Wiley, 1958.

5. Miller, S. M., and Elliot G. Mishler. "Social Class, Mental Illness and American Psychiatry: An Expository Review," in *Mental Health of the Poor, op. cit.,* pp. 16–36.

Part Two

Schools
and the Poor

Chapter Four

The Middle-Class Aura

Little Red Schoolhouse
(a view from Spanish Harlem)

School stunk. I hated school and all its
teachers. I hated the crispy look of the
teachers and the draggy-long hours they
took out of my life from nine to three-
thirty. I dug being outside no matter what
kind of weather. Only chumps worked
and studied.

Piri Thomas. From Down These Mean
Streets, *by Piri Thomas, Alfred A. Knopf,
Inc., New York, 1967, p. 70.*

The poor of our country are required to attend school. The school becomes a second home. It becomes the primary indoctrinating force for many of the values of our society. The school spends, for example, a good deal of its energy on creating and enforcing standards of personal appearance for its students. Theoretically, these standards represent the desires and the values of the populace; they may actually be more representative of the positions of the school principals or superintendents. (For example, in one school district such codes of dress include the requirement that a girl's dress be no more than one inch above the knee, in some others, that its hem touch the floor when the girl is kneeling; prohibit the boys from wearing T-shirts to school; require the boys to wear their hair appropriately short, and to refrain from lengthening their side-burns; prohibit the girls from wearing patent-leather shoes for fear the boys will see under their dresses in the reflections, etc.)

Such are the ways that our schools act as guardians of our society's values and morals. Dress is, of course, an obvious and a controversial example. Other societal values are infinitely more subtle, more fundamental to our teachers' life styles, and more pernicious in degrading and humiliating young people who are somehow nonconforming. . . . In this chapter we shall consider those covert and influential, pervasive, ingrained parochial attitudes of our schools and their ministers, described in some quarters as the *middle-class aura.*

The Values of Our Teachers

It should be noted at the outset that middle-classness itself should not be viewed negatively, except as it reflects the narrow notion that it is somehow favored as a life style. If we were able to stand back and say "To be a middle-class American is one of the many ways to 'be' in this world," middle-classness might gain a new perspective. We might recognize a middle-class value system as one with unique and often delightfully positive traits; or as one which, in David Riesman's terms, is hopelessly other-directed, competitive, insensitive, acquisitive. How we label it most likely depends upon where *we* are in relation to it.

The typical American teacher, whatever the color of his skin, is middle-class. An anthropologist who had lived and worked with Indians of the Southwest recently told me that by the time an Indian man or woman has gone through our school system and becomes a teacher himself, he is no longer an Indian. Being an Indian is a way of life. To get the necessary grades to make it in college today, a person would have to conform to the American order—and in so doing he develops a certain way of life—in a word, he becomes middle-class.

We noted earlier that the term *middle class* should not necessarily be viewed negatively. But middle-class people generally consider theirs as the favored life style. Middle-class Americans see others who are different as somehow badly different. Evidence of this is apparent repeatedly when Americans travel abroad. Our tourists travel halfway across the world to find a hotel with a familiar name and to order prime ribs, rare. . . .

The point is, whether we like it or not, that the economic affluence the average American has experienced (including the teacher) has engendered in him a great attachment to his way of life, and has left him with very little tolerance for behavioral or cultural difference. He has been nurtured on a diet of America's assets: America has never lost a war, America is the great melting pot of the world, America elects its officials democratically, American know-how has put the world on wheels, America is first in space, America's buildings are the tallest, her rivers the longest, her canyons the grandest, and her cities the largest in the world. It is only recently that our young people have found out that our air is becoming polluted, our rivers congested and foul,* (5) our national attitudes toward war and peace widely criticized, our ventures into space dramatic but wasteful, our culture narrow and intolerant, and our pace frantic.

Perhaps it is time to reorder our priorities. What about a high ranking for such values as: our children are the happiest, our people the most tranquil, our families the most closely knit, our neighbors the friendliest, our teenagers the most accepted, our elderly the most useful, our urban centers the most habitable and efficient, and our culture among the most tolerant of the cultures of the world?

But what if our measure of a "great" society got *completely* outside of its middle-class bag? What if it discarded its yardstick of evaluations of good or bad by some external criterion? And what if it then just tried to become as great as it might become, measured against only its own potential? Our achievements as a people might seem considerably less glamorous if we measured them against what they *might* be!

Middle-classness, then, has come to mean not only a style of living, but a way of believing about others and other styles of living. Middle-classness itself must be judged by that part of the world which has retained (or developed) a reverence for humankind that transcends

---

* Dr. Edward D. Goldberg, a chemist of Scripps Institute of Oceanography in La Jolla, California, was quoted in the *Christian Science Monitor* (January 21, 1969) as saying: "The United States, in comparison with the rest of the world, appears to be responsible for around one-third to one-half of many of the contaminants introduced into the atmosphere or oceans."

acquisitive success or technological perfection. The implications for that judgment run deep into the nature of man and his role in group living, and reflect back to John Collier's thoughts cited earlier: that man must turn again to the Indian for the secrets of human joy, love, reverence for life, and oneness with nature.

We have used the term *middle class* to describe America's vast middle group, a culture of great complexity and appeal but which also carries with it a certain chauvinism or superpatriotism that disallows difference. To the extent that this saturates much of middle-class America, it is a fair and accurate statement. There are other traits of middle-classness, not necessarily biased in nature, but equally powerful in influencing people subtly and coercively. We shall discuss two of these: the notions of *routine* and *evaluation*.

Americans tend to have a penchant for routine. The "on-time" syndrome is supposed to be prejudicial to peoples of other cultures who do not rank punctuality high on their value scale. Yet one would have to search far and wide to find any person of any culture who is not present at an event which is highly and personally significant to him, *at the time* that event occurs, so long as the knowledge of time is available to him. It is the nature of an event, not a generalized belief about time, that influences one's promptness.

In our schools, teachers and administrators demand that their students arrive on time. It is not that anything so particularly significant occurs within the first few minutes after nine o'clock. It is rather that to be there on time conforms with the routine, and all children must conform with the routine. Subtly then, we say to a student who does not arrive on time, "You are different and you are wrong," while overtly we say, "You are not punctual." The student, and especially the culturally different student, finds very little reason to arrive exactly on time since that time is invariably taken up with other perplexing routines: saluting the flag (the exact meaning of which has never been explained and totally escapes even the acculturated children); calling the roll (when the teacher can easily see that a desk which he *routinely* assigned to a given student is empty); or reading "the thought for the day" from the board (which is invariably the teacher's thought and often either a mystery to the student, or a totally specious parable about equality or brotherhood that in our ghetto areas the school itself belies).

The myriad routines that some of our teachers continue to demand of our children (all in the name of order and control) bore them, dull them, pledge them to conformity, and extinguish their creativity. The routine of lining up before entering or leaving a room is another example of activity which is not understood by the students and not explained by the teachers. It has come to represent little more than homage to routine and is a legacy of an earlier, even more doctrinaire day.

Indeed, one creative and liberated first-grade teacher recently illustrated to me the inanity of arbitrary lining up for each change of locale. He explained to his six-year-olds the rationale that the parents and teachers were worried that children would get hurt if they pushed or shoved while trying to get to lunch or recess, and so most teachers have their children line up and move out in order. He then asked them if they thought the class needed to line up or if they understood the rules well enough without that routine. (The *rule,* after all, is not that children line up, but rather that they pass from place to place in an orderly way.) The children not only decided against lining up, but as might be generalized from this one example, were so caught up in the excitement of the way this teacher had structured his classroom, that they often failed to hear the passing bell! In fact, on more than one occasion, I have observed the teacher reminding students that the bell has rung and that they could resume their activity after lunch. This teacher had managed somehow to allow for differences and to encourage reasoning in his classroom, and was able to escape from the *routine* reflex that dominates many of our schools.

Another middle-class trait which silently but ubiquitously operates among our teachers is the notion (it is really much more than a notion—it is really a powerful and primary drive in our culture) that all of the children need constantly to be evaluated. Our society is remarkably, if not uniquely, judgmental.

Indeed, in his research in factoring out the meanings implicit in our use of language, Osgood has cited the Evaluative Factor (i.e., encompassing the polar adjectives *good–bad*) as easily the most dominant of all the dimensions of meaning. (7) Said another way, we tend to impose a good or bad meaning upon most of the experiences in our lives. Our teachers, of course, merely reflect in school the heavy cultural emphasis of the larger community upon judging, measuring, rewarding, and last but obviously not least, punishing.

A tragic by-product of our American middle-class trait of judging everything is that, on the scale we use, our minorities within the system—our people of little power—find themselves evaluated repeatedly and remarkably low. Looked at in a broader sense, this means that they are constantly, if not deliberately, being punished. As has been noted earlier, the psychological impact of this constant negative bombardment becomes overwhelming to the self-concept of any individual. (Indeed, we need not look only to our minorities to find punishment used to degrade and humiliate; it is, sadly enough, a rather standard tool of many of our carefully trained and constantly in-control teachers.)

If we visit almost any classroom of younger children, we find that the line that is straightest moves out first; the crooked line goes last. We find the window monitor being chosen from among those who "can sit up the tallest." We find the row whose children all have their hands folded getting to go to the blackboard. The child who calls out and does not raise his hand does not get to recite. The child who talks to his neighbor instead of studying gets moved to an isolated spot near the teacher's desk.

The public school classroom is replete with examples of direct and indirect punishment, the latter being possibly the more damaging. As a psychological consultant to an elementary school district, I was constantly suggesting to teachers that they include, not exclude, a given child who was overly garrulous. (Indeed, to isolate him served solely to punish him but not at all to administer to his needs to learn through verbal interaction, which were obviously stronger than average.) That they offer monitorships to the psychologically least secure, not to the most conforming or the self-assured. That the straightness of lines or the uniformity of rows has little to do with education, and that, stripped of their rationalizations, such routines tend to be arbitrary and artificial opportunities for some children to be judged and to fail.

From the meager samples cited above, one can imagine that if an acculturated, self-assured Anglo child must contend with (and finds himself threatened by) such constant challenges to his beliefs about himself and to his logical and natural way of behaving, the powerless child of a minority culture must indeed feel helpless and lost.

Our schools deal primarily in external evaluation, (2) but then so does our culture. The great tragedy is not that a culture very logically tries to pass on its traits to its young, but that one of the influential traits of this culture is its exclusivity.

A significant piece of research was conducted recently which pointed to some disturbing factors about teachers. Rosenthal and Jacobson studied the notion that poor children fall behind in school because it is indeed what their teachers expect. (8)

In this work, teachers were asked to describe classroom behavior of their children at the end of the academic year. Children who were expected to grow intellectually (by the teachers) were also described (by the teachers) as being happier, more curious, more interesting than the other children, and were seen as more appealing, better adjusted, and more affectionate.

Interestingly, many of the children for whom teachers did not hold high expectations also grew intellectually, but the more they grew, the less favorably they were rated.

Thus, children who were expected to progress intellectually were also perceived as more estimable personalities by their teachers. In fact, the study showed that the most unfavorable ratings were applied to children in low-ability classrooms who actually gained the *most* intellectually.

In seeking reasons for the teachers' perceptions of low-track children as less adjusted and potentially unsuccessful students, the researchers concluded that the subtle aspects of tone of voice, facial expression, touch, and posture represent ways in which the teacher communicates her expectations. The child, then, receives this communication and very possibly incorporates it into his own self-concept, motivation, expectations, and way of behaving. The researchers conclude by suggesting that all the crash programs geared toward the children might better be focused upon the teachers and their attitudes.

In another major investigation, Ryans conducted 100 separate research projects over a six-year period, and used over 6000 teachers in attempting to ascertain the characteristics of good and not-so-good teachers. One key finding he presented was that the good teachers *had attitudes that were favorable to pupils.* (9) In other words, they appreciated the children they were teaching, and tended to believe in them and their motives.

Still another commentary which is pertinent here was made by Kenneth B. Clark, based on a questionnaire distributed in Central Harlem in 1963. Clark concluded that Central Harlem youth were falling below their grade levels in ever-increasing numbers because ". . . substandard performance is expected of them." (1) He went on to indict teachers, principals, and the community for this situation. And in the same area, an outspoken minister has added that the primary problem in the ghetto schools ". . . is one of attitude, which expresses itself in low expectations on the part of the middle-class teachers whose concept of a human being is not met by these children." (4)

We have, of course, been saying much the same thing. (More of this in Part Three.) In fact, we have broadened our hypothesis to include the notion that our teachers are culturally conditioned to expect and to insist upon certain desired ways of responding and behaving. The values of our teachers are such that they demand conformity to routine, that youngsters are evaluated externally and often, and that obedience and "good" behavior rank most highly in our classroom scale of desiderata.

A final point must be made here that will, we hope, place the above statement in a certain perspective. The term *middle class* carries with it an assumption that people who represent such a category have at least a minimal level of power. Our typical middle-class teachers are Americans who feel adequately powerful about themselves and their abilities. The minority children, the culturally different who are in our schools, feel strangely helpless in the presence of the powerful authority figure of the teacher, demanding conformity to the tenets of his value system. Our public schools, then, instead of motivating and encouraging students from poverty or other subcultures, successfully inhibit them. Only in recent years has the awareness appeared that permits the use of the phrase, "the school push-out" in lieu of the phrase "the school drop-out." What different connotations these two have. . . .

Recognition for the Powerless

American students who are powerless have impaired opportunity to receive recognition. The structure of our schools is such that recognition is afforded those who somehow have won something, are highly skilled at something, or have behaved in a certain way. It is not the intent here to criticize these grounds for recognition; a society has the right to establish the criteria it wishes to reward. But the specific interpretations of those criteria serve further to illustrate the narrowness of acceptable patterns of behavior in our society. Recognition is given for success at tasks that are heavily loaded toward middle-class abilities. Non-middle-class achievements bring little reward, are forbidden, in certain schools, and are perceived as useless or degrading in others. Some examples should serve to illustrate the contrast.

Typically, in our secondary schools, certain students are rewarded handsomely in print and through travel for having unusual communication skills in debate and forensics. It is certain that such skills rank highly with most Americans and their reward is laudable. But might we also consider another form of communication as intrinsically valuable, deserving of remarkable reward, and somehow hauntingly aesthetic as well? What about dance—the intricate, rhythmical, and often highly personal expression of one's self through movement! Such an expression just might, ultimately, bring people into close human encounters which plain verbal interaction cannot approach. Yet most of our schools tolerate, at best, such wild configurations and more likely will restrict them to certain locales or times—let alone offer any kind of recognition for the creators or participants. Some dance is, of course, the respectable kind, such as modern or ballet, and students half-way skilled in these modes of expression are given center stage on occasion. It is the indigenous dance of today's urban student, which like a gay kaleidoscope decorates the center-city, that brings forth the reactionary regulations, the erect posture edicts, the "hands should be confined to proper positions" memos. . . .

Our schools typically reward students who learn well the material in, for example, an American history class. Success is usually measured by absorption of a textbook. If most textbooks on American history were carefully analyzed, one would come away rather shockingly convinced that all Americans ever engaged in were wars, politics, and commerce. Indeed, even the last-named is seldom presented in terms of the creativity or the inventiveness of people in a frontier era, but rather their opportunism, their aggressiveness, their shrewdness (with the "savages" for the most part).

A major part of our *real* history, of course, has to do with the quality and variety of life styles to be found here. But these areas seem virtually to be ignored in our texts in favor of various series of events such as how Americans clobbered the British (twice!), the Indians, the French, the Spanish, the Germans and Japanese, and more recently, the North Koreans. Our texts emphasize the diplomacy of our presidents, not their personalities or the people they surrounded themselves with. (An exception to this is Lincoln, who somehow embodies the secret wish of all Americans for every president past and future; the once poor man with the indomitable drive to succeed, with courage, with industry, with honesty, with common sense, with earthiness—in short, with the typical American ethic.)

By giving the better grades to those students who do best on exams based upon the textbooks described above, the system is obviously rewarding its students for perceiving history in a given way. If a student balks at such a view—for any one of many reasons: no identification with the all-white characters, an abhorrence of war and violence, a primary concern with the aesthetics of American life, an interest in the history of people *out* of the mainstream, people like himself, who live in ghettoes—if a student looks for other things in his American history class, his grade reflects his "incompetence" or his lack of subordination. Indeed, the only recognition he receives is negative.

English classes too reflect middle-class bias. This is not to say that there must be adulation for poor grammar, gutter language, or inept communication. But, in our public schools, the above categorizations have become confused with unabashed bias against accents, tone, slang, style, and new or colorful expressions. Minority youngsters are made ashamed of the only mode of expression they know. Small wonder that many become morose and sullen and will not volunteer to express themselves.

On rare occasions imaginative teachers have encouraged—through, for example, dramatics—minority children to write and perform skits in their own idiom. The audiences are their peers, and their communicative skills are roundly appreciated. Thus they *are* recognized for what they *can* do.

The key to effective performance in English classes ought to be the extent to which a student can communicate—in whatever style he knows—rather than that he conform to any one style or any given teacher's particular demands. The colorful modes of expression, the coining of new phrases, the constant evolution of language ought to be enjoyed and welcomed among our teachers. Indeed, such innovative uses of language ought to receive recognition!

Some teachers of language feel that, given encouragement and a feeling of adequacy about his expressive abilities, the culturally different student will reach for more universal ways of communicating; he will indeed educate himself in the communicative skills.

There is one other arena where our middle-class bias dominates which deserves attention here. That is the popular and presumably democratic institution known as student government.

The Game of Student Government

Virtually every secondary school and many elementary schools in our country go through the *routine* of organizing a student government. Presumably the leaders represent the students and have power to implement policy. But in reality, much of the student government activity is a game—and the student leaders find that out rather quickly.

The leaders soon find that they have no power to make policy, only to carry it out, and even then, only when the school administration agrees that it should be carried out. In many instances, student leaders have attempted to bring to a campus assembly speakers who have something relevant and controversial to say—only to be vetoed by the principal on some vague reference to "the Board, downtown."

Mature guidance, however, has its place, too, as the following incident shows. A young teacher, intent upon adhering to the philosophy of self-government, allowed her second-grade class to adjudicate their own classroom problems. When one youngster broke a class-made rule repeatedly, he was brought before the jury. The child was found guilty of the infraction, and when sentencing time came, the jury pronounced that he should be "punished by being shot." The teacher was able, through persuasion and clarification, to amend the ruling to include ". . . with a water gun."

It is rather clear that children need adult guidance. Yet a distinction must be made between guidance and control, between facilitating self-government and manipulating "puppet" leaders.

In the outskirts of a large city in California there are a barrio of Mexican-Americans, a ghetto of Negroes, and an enclave of whites, all of which feed the same high school and two junior highs. One of these junior high schools has a population that is virtually equal in representation from the three groups. As such, it could be considered, in physical terms, an integrated school. Psychologically, and in terms of the relative power of each group, it still functions as an arm of our society's caste system, if not by ethnic differentiation, then certainly by cultural.

Student governments at this school have, until recently, reflected almost exclusively one segment of the student body: the achieving, industrious, conforming, obedient, middle-class student. Officers in the Student Council have always been elected (one from each home room) by their classmates, but only if they had met the requirements of (1) a certain grade-point average, and (2) a certain merit score on behavior.

Such requirements are clearly system-serving and are, in a sense, discriminatory against a large segment of the school population. Those students who are, for example, bilingual, rebellious against the controlled curriculum, more rural in their backgrounds, etc., cannot serve in student government—nor are they represented by the others.

Not long ago this school's administration recognized the growing tension and division in its student body * and implemented a dual track system of student government. One track continues to be the Student Council, elected as described above. The other track is the Human Relations Advisory Council, elected by the student body and requiring no standards of achievement or conformity; representatives are selected on the basis of popularity. With these two bodies working jointly, more segments of the student body are represented. Said another way, positions of power have been created in this institution so that previously powerless members could now find identity, redress, and communication.

The failure of student government in many schools has been directly related to that body's becoming an arm of the administration; in sociological terms, student body officers become "confirming others." They are chosen according to criteria which ensure their agreement with the policies and procedures of the dominant group.

---

* Activist students, both in college and high school, in a quest for a share of the power to influence their own educations, have stirred and awakened not only the students but also the faculty and administrators of the public school system throughout California and certainly in other parts of the country.

Their intolerance of diversity and their lack of qualification to represent the less powerful members of the student body illustrate rather sharply their saturation with the "middle-class aura."

Friedenberg, in his classic, *The Vanishing Adolescent,* (3) has noted that the sham of democracy which characterizes much of our secondary school student government has added to the aimlessness and purposelessness of our adolescent population.

The problem exists everywhere, but it is especially acute for minorities. They can only feel that they have any attachment to an institution if somehow they see a way to influence that institution. Again, identification becomes attached to power, the power that came from a sense of control over one's destiny.

Earl Kelley, in an excellent little book, *In Defense of Youth,* (6) tried to tell us several years ago that what we set up as the ideal for our economic and political society (however poorly we sometimes implement it) ought to be the ideal for our educational institutions. If we believe in democracy, why don't we believe in it in our schools? That we do not implement our democracy so well in our society at large is a further sign of the middle-class tendency to be exclusive. Of course, this is reflected in our schools. . . .

American society has the highest standard of living in the world. Its middle class is the backbone of its affluence and is its largest cultural and economic group. As such, it typifies dominance, power, superiority, exclusivity. There is an aura of attitude and of style that goes with being a middle-class American. One salient characteristic is a penchant for evangelism, a wish to make the world over in the American middle-class image. Our schools perpetuate this evangelical fervor—sometimes deliberately, more often unknowingly. There is no room for the deviant.

Political activity has historically been the means of redress and expression in America. In the chapter which follows, we shall explore the potentials of the political scene for people who are seeking power—including the politics of education.

Notes

1. Clark, Kenneth, quoted in Patricia Cayo Sexton. *Spanish Harlem.* New York: Harper, 1965, p. 60.

2. Ebel, Robert L., and John H. Suehr. "The Continuing Debate: To Mark or Not to Mark," in Don E. Hamachek, editor, *Human Dynamics in Psychology and Education.* Boston: Allyn and Bacon, 1968, pp. 288–302.

3. Friedenberg, Edgar Z. *The Vanishing Adolescent*. Boston: Beacon, 1959.

4. Galamison, Reverend Milton. Quoted in *Spanish Harlem, op. cit.,* p. 61.

5. Goldberg, Edward D. Speech at 135th meeting of the American Association for the Advancement of Science, Dallas, January, 1969.

6. Kelley, Earl C. *In Defense of Youth*. Englewood Cliffs, N.J.: Prentice-Hall, 1962.

7. Osgood, Charles E., George J. Suci, and Percy H. Tannenbaum. *The Measurement of Meaning*. Urbana, Ill.: University of Illinois Press, 1957.

8. Rosenthal, Robert, and Lenore F. Jacobson. *Pygmalion in the Classroom; Teacher Expectation and Pupils' Intellectual Development*. New York: Holt, Rinehart and Winston, 1968.

9. Ryans, D. G. "Some Relationships between Pupil Behavior and Certain Teacher Characteristics," *Journal of Educational Psychology,* 52, 1961, pp. 82–91.

Chapter Five

Power, Politics, and the Poor

Dream Deferred

What happens to a dream deferred?

      Does it dry up
like a raisin in the sun?
Or fester like a sore—
      And then run?
Does it stink like rotten meat?
Or crust and sugar over—
      like a syrupy sweet?
      Maybe it just sags
      like a heavy load.
      Or does it explode?

American schools are in a revolution. In the high schools and colleges it is student-led and, on occasion, teacher-led. On the elementary level, the parents are waving the banners and picket signs and protesting to the Boards of Education. There is general discontent. Political conservatives ask why their tax dollars are so wickedly wasted. Progressives decry the lack of political and economic support for new programs and burgeoning student bodies.

Teachers complain about crowded classrooms, poor remuneration, and inadequate supplies and equipment. There is ample evidence of the deterioration of inner-city education: decaying structures, inadequately trained teachers, poor technical facilities, general overcrowding. Lingering prejudice and bigotry often still prevail. Jonathan Kozol, in his *Death at an Early Age,* (8) shocked America with his candid exposé of the schooling offered to black children in the Boston area as late as the middle 1960s.

It would be nice to simply choose between two polar solutions to our educational troubles. We could say either, (1) "If you want quality education you have to pay for it," or (2) "We must bring education under closer government scrutiny and controls." But the problem is more complex.

We can learn from some of our young activists. Part of their methodology repels us; their demands raise our hackles; their language affronts us. But their message stirs our consciences. They are alerting us to danger signs in our system. They are calling for a *real* participatory democracy in the schools. They are shaming us for our failure to manifest it in our educational enterprise.

Let us examine some of the moves toward revolutions that have been initiated by the powerless people of America. Thanks to the commitment of some defiant, often tactless, but generally courageous young people, the poor of our society today are touched with sparks of hope. But we must not make too much of that hope unless the tentative efforts made thus far can really take hold. What chances have they for success?

The Poor Have Learned What We Have Taught Them

The poor have generally rejected the curriculum officially established for them in the public schools. It is not a conscious rejection; more likely it is due to the incongruity of school with life outside the classroom. The latter is so pervasive that the former does not have a chance. In the words of an old black grandmother from the heart of Harlem, describing her wayward grandson, "The street's done got Rodney!" (2)

In fact, the poor have learned a lot from the dominant culture, as has been seen in recent college and high school disorders. The poor have learned well the establishment game of welfare. Why would they not be expected to learn well the game of pressure, the game of coercion, the game of violence?

A sociologist studying the incidence of racial prejudice among professional athletes (1) questioned a well-known black sports personality about his contacts with the police. The athlete told him that while he was driving through a swanky part of town in his new Cadillac, a police officer pulled him over. Not knowing for sure what he had done wrong, the man began to take out his driver's license. The policeman approached his car, told him to get out and ordered him to place his hands on the roof of his car while the officer frisked him. The man wanted to avoid an incident, so he obeyed.

In another situation a young, dark-skinned Jamaican described how, when he lived in an elegant apartment on the west side of town, he was stopped by police 34 times in one year. He finally succumbed to the harassment and moved to a ghetto.

It is safe to say that many who read these words have been stopped by traffic police, but certainly few have ever experienced a frisking or the humiliation of being confronted as a criminal.

Compare the above incidents with another that occurred in a college in the fall of 1968. A group of militant black students, only recently out of the ghetto, "took over" portions of the administration building in a virtually all-white, all middle-class suburban institution. Their aim was to hold dialogue from a position of power with the college president. One of the demands they made was that all personnel being detained (myself included) put their hands up against the wall and be frisked. Where did these students learn such tactics?

As one reads Frantz Fanon (*The Wretched of the Earth*), (3) the inescapable comparison emerges between the natives in colonial Africa resorting to whatever tactics they must to rid themselves of their captors, and the Black Students' Unions on our campuses proudly taking their freedom "by any means necessary." Typically unalert and unsuspecting, college administrations habitually underestimate the student leaders; they fail to realize that the students too have read Fanon—and Malcolm X and Stokely Carmichael and Eldridge Cleaver.

The poor have been learning for years that the powerful members of our society have a great deal of force behind them. But, they have also observed that force need not always be used—merely the threat of it often suffices. Indeed, in the "takeover" described above, little actual force was used; yet the sheer number of supporters, the menacing looks, the cold and humorless voices, and the intimidation served much the same purpose.

While our poor have not learned well the details of world history or of American political achievements, they seem to have realized with brilliance the lessons of international intrigue and of our own industrial unions. A major tenet of industrial collective bargaining is that one must only negotiate from a position of strength. A vertical relationship (with one protagonist having an obvious upper hand) is always a discriminatory one. Hence our poor today have begun to establish themselves in horizontal relationships with any institution they confront. They refuse, for example, to be outnumbered in any dialogue. They often put on a display of physical strength, such as having several escorts accompany a speaker or a leader. They speak with condescension and disdain of the officials of the institution, thus psychologically enhancing their own self-images. And they often present demands and positions that seem perfectly outrageous and irresponsible to the opposition; but while they refuse to mention compromise, the extreme initial position they take is established on the fulcrum of compromise—rare is the session that closes with the militant student worse off than before he started.

What the system must learn from the poor (who originally learned it from us) is that positions of power must be created within organizations (schools, colleges, unions, service and professional groups) for people of diverse cultures. As black students, for example, see black people in positions of power in their schools, the conventional avenues of redress and communication suddenly seem less hopeless. They have a way to go. They need not clash violently with the administration to have their needs considered. . . .

The major militancy being exhibited by the poor is among the black poor. And even among blacks, only a minority is active. Yet the power structure had better not deceive itself into thinking that the ". . . good people of the poor community are home wringing their hands at the damage caused by these militants." It is far more likely that the bulk of the poor may be publicly admonishing their brothers for unruly tactics, while privately they watch each episode muttering through their teeth, "Give it to 'em, brother."

The warning signs are in fact coming from all corners of the nation and from diverse spokesmen. One such warning was couched recently in a most disarming title: "The Gentle Revolutionary." This article in *West Magazine* (a segment of the *Los Angeles Times*) was written by a Mexican-American college professor, Ralph Guzman. Guzman writes:

The Brown Power Mexican is telling the Anglo that things have changed. The Mexican rural laborer faded away a generation ago. His son moved to the city. He's young, tough, smart, and he's watching you, white man. He's not patient, he's not submissive. He's not *Tio Taco* who wants to please his Anglo *patrón*. (4)

A leader of the United Mexican-American Students (UMAS) at a west coast college recently explained that "Our people have a residual of a very powerful religion holding rein on them. If we as student leaders are to retain that support we must as yet operate within the acceptable boundaries of that religion. But if that religion holds our people down then we will break through—and our people *must* come with us."

Across the country in New York City, a young mustachioed Puerto Rican told this writer how he sat across the table from Mayor John Lindsay and *told* him what had to be done if the city was to have peace.

Even the skin-brothers of the power structure, the white poor, are beginning to rally together. The National Organizing Committee (NOC), with national offices in Chicago, was formed in September 1968, with the express aim of organizing white students who come from the working class; among their demands are the lowering of the voting age to 18 and restructuring of the schools to emphasize working-class history. The white poor, who have solely the cultural difference as their "handicap," are learning the techniques of rebellion from the black poor.

A final lesson that the racalcitrant poor have learned so well from us is that when change is needed, the pressure must be applied directly at the top. The young militant student refuses to be put off by the teacher or the professor saying, "I don't have the power to do that." He moves with dispatch to the principal or president and sets forth his demands. And if the school head is restricted by Boards of Education or Trustees or Regents, the students make it clear that they hold *him* responsible for convincing the Board of the need for change. In some instances, the demands are presented directly to the Board.

Shocking as this intimidation appears to be to most of us, it smacks most heavily of the kind of political lobbying (economic pressuring) that goes on in state capitols and in Washington. . . .

For most good-hearted, liberal Americans, a lingering affection for an earlier approach which said We are all brothers, we do not

Power, Pride, and the Integration Hang-up

recognize or discriminate on the basis of black or white, complicates today's social turmoil. The above stance continues to have appeal to vast numbers of Americans. To others, it has finally become the accepted alternative. Sad, and interesting too, that violence or its imminence have convinced some Americans that such an alternative is a better one.

But because of the powerful and residual pull of the integration and brotherhood approach, even the tolerant and open-minded middle-class citizens of our country find it difficult to understand what is happening today. They fail to comprehend that pride can only come from self-implementation. They fail to distinguish between real integration and the standard kind of assimilation that has gone on regularly.

Consider the following vignette: In the early spring of 1969, a junior college held a convocation to discuss aspects of campus rebellion that had been near but not at their campus. They invited, among others, a black student from a nearly four-year institution to explain aspects of his militancy. This student was a freshman, straight out of a ghetto, in college just over five months. He brought seven of his friends with him, all of whom were freshmen and recent ghetto residents, who took up positions around the stage and at the wing exits. He spoke with confidence and defiance. His friends stood proudly, arms crossed and heads high. They stared over the crowd of 500. There was unmistakable power in their bearing.

Two attitudes were later expressed by members of the audience. One asked, "How could they have become so duped, so violent, so disruptive in less than half a year of exposure to college?" The other seemed to say, "How remarkable that in less than six months these students could have developed such pride in themselves and in their people!" Of course, an analysis of those six months would have shown dormitory living where 800 whites shared a building with 100 blacks; where two cultures, one heavily influenced by poverty and powerlessness, lived side by side but did *not* intermingle; where some of the separation was deliberately influenced by leaders of the Black Students' Union. The dismay of the white liberal would be hard to describe concerning psychological apartheid of that physically integrated dormitory. But the question which remains is, could the standard kind of integration as we have always known it have provided a sense of worth or identity to black, formerly poor and degraded Americans? Perhaps *only* the solidarity of a hundred brothers and sisters around him could give the black student his pride.

I would say that a valid and useful integration did occur at that dormitory. Earlier it was noted that some good people cannot differentiate between superficial assimilation and real integration. Real integration would be based upon the notion that America is a culturally pluralistic society. If we are indeed pluralistic, then we must tolerate and encourage the juxtaposition of diverse life styles and cultures. Integration then might very well mean black people living in a cluster side-by-side with a cluster of Anglos and *not* actually intermixing. For although intermixing does not occur, a kind of multicultural educational process goes on. The extent to which intermixing occurs is the extent to which each culture loses some of its identity. This is not to say that such a loss of uniqueness is bad in any absolute sense. But if such erosion of a given culture is to be avoided, then an integration of the kind defined above may be the only answer. Of course, such an integration can only exist if there is a mutual recognition of the pride and the power of each group for each other.

I think Dr. Martin Luther King, Jr., understood this idea of pluralistic integration as he moved through the final metamorphoses in his own thinking. In the last article written by King (published after his death) in the early spring of 1968, he noted that ". . . once again we must reaffirm our belief in building a democratic society, in which blacks and whites can live together as brothers, where we will all come to see that integration is not a problem, but an opportunity to participate in the beauty of diversity." (7)

Lest the reader wonder why in this writing I have focused on integration, ostensibly a black-white issue, it must be repeated that the integration being considered is a cultural one, and in American society one must be most often concerned with the affluent and dominant culture that does not integrate with the several cultures that are less powerful.

Though with darker-skinned people there was always an exception, integration has actually been the way in America. But the classic American integration (and that which creates the "hang-up" for well-meaning people today) has, virtually without exception in relation to white-skinned peoples, assumed that varying cultures would integrate *into* the dominant American life-pattern. Some rub-off, to be sure, would invariably exist, so that French and Greek and German restaurants, certain speech patterns or phrases, and certain influences of dress and dance and hair style would sustain some diversity. But integration chiefly meant assimilation—and with most immigrants, agreeably so.

The hang-up comes with the emerging appreciation among black Americans (and Puerto Ricans and Mexican-Americans) for their own pattern of cultural living, and their reluctance to give it up. A truly pluralistic integration must value the many cultural varieties which exist within it without dilution.

Further, I would say that the public school plan for integration which has been most applauded and which, through a rocky start and many setbacks, continues to maintain a positive prognosis (the Berkeley Plan), may not be integration at all, in the old, now commonly accepted definition of the word. Rather, it may be the proto-nation of its procedures and objectives should prove useful.

type of the kind of pluralistic integration described above. An exami-

A Pluralistic Integration

In September of 1968, Berkeley, California, a city with a school population of 51 percent white, 41 percent Negro, 7 percent Oriental, and 1 percent "other," engaged in a plan of total "integration" of its public schools. It involved two-way busing, complete in-service teacher reeducation, and massive community involvement and participation.

The public news media, in their standard usage of the term "integration," have already misled the general population; people now presume about Berkeley, as they always have about integration, that the plan consisted of the physical mixing of the races within any given school. It did that, but it did much more.

In Berkeley there was a concerted attempt to create a social entity in each classroom that might represent the desired, democratic social entity of the outside environment. This meant classroom composition was based upon sexual, racial, academic, and economic variables; it required consideration for a curriculum that reflected many cultural and personal differences; it permitted, even encouraged, language variances, expression of unique styles of music, art, humor, dance, etc.; and it respected a variety of home backgrounds. This microcosm necessarily required democratic classrooms and a faculty and community that participated with interest and influence in all aspects of the educational enterprise.

In describing how the Berkeley residents were able to communicate well enough to create a plan based upon such mutual respect, one writer stated:

The acceptance of such a far-reaching plan can be explained only by depicting the preceding decade of intense community confrontation. The key to this confrontation is that it was "integrated"—that the community —and particularly blacks and whites—were talking to each other, though quite often shouting. . . . And it was through working together in such "encounter grouping" that Negroes and whites developed sufficient trust in each other to demand that their children also participate in a genuine school community. (5)

It would almost seem that, from a political perspective, the phase of confrontation, tension, and pressure is a necessary one before barriers can be lowered enough for significant dialogue to occur.

The busing format of the Berkeley Plan is in itself unique: Regardless of home address, all children in the district who are in kindergarten through third grade attend the formerly heavily white schools, and all children who are in fourth through sixth grade attend the formerly heavily black schools.

Another rare aspect of the Berkeley endeavor is that nearly a thousand outside community people contribute to the educational process. One hundred aides, mostly black, work in what is called "cluster teaching," in helping to uplift the self-images and learning confidence of the black children. Some members of the black community in Berkeley have pointed out that what is being attempted there is in many ways an indictment of the entire American elementary education system. No child, they have pointed out, was getting a good education. No child was experiencing a schooling that was relevant to today's social alignments. The pluralistic classroom in Berkeley is one attempt to correct that situation. The Berkeley Plan offers an integration which is acceptable to militant blacks today who scoff at the word and its commonly accepted implication.

Integration at Berkeley is an example of cultural juxtaposition, with mutual respect for all cultures involved and without attempting to diminish or absorb one culture into another. Basic to such a condition is the total commitment to and final influence of the community upon the schools. Community influence and community control emerge today as necessary preconditions for effective education. Why? What does community control really involve?

Most problems between the poor and the affluent, as they come together (or fail to) in our schools, are in the larger urban centers of the country. This is partly because the central authority in an overly large school district tends to address its energies to a kind of "mythical middle," to a dominant group which may not really exist.

What sufficed as an organizational pattern and a focus for governing boards when the district had a handful of schools is totally unworkable with the galaxy of schools each city currently must operate. It is becoming increasingly apparent that a decentralized administrative

The Community and the School

structure is a necessary element of relevant education. This also means an application at a more local and a more manageable level of curricular offerings, of instructional assignments, of teacher evaluation, and of individualized programs.

The sad state of the matter is that when school boards address their energy toward perpetuating the culture they currently enjoy, they are in reality being irrelevant even to their own middle-class sons and daughters who have moved so far. Societies are fluid; they are dynamic. Institutions must be structured with flexibility and established *for* change.

The Berkeley Plan illustrated the remarkable advantages of community involvement in education—provided the groundwork is appropriately laid and sometimes intense human interaction is anticipated. Often our twentieth-century perspective about education gets muddled—we operate as if the family were miraculously freed of any involvement with the growth and development of its children because that is the school's job. But education does not occur five hours out of the day and then stop. The more profound education (cogitation, agitation, encountering) occurs outside of the classroom. Education is everyone's business all the time.

The way it is now, schools do not and cannot communicate with the public—and the public has little access to school policy-making or implementation. The anonymity of public education alienates its constituency. Decisions are made about a school and its activities years away and miles removed from the needs of that school, and even the changes that are demanded through the emerging political awareness of once powerless people can often be inadequate and ineffectual because the articulation, the problem, and the power are so distant from each other.

One report from California recently cited much greater gains for youngsters through compensatory education programs in smaller school districts than in large urban school districts. While the implementation of the programs was comparable in both situations, in the smaller districts the participation of parents, friends, and relatives in the new programs was much more visible to the students. The school ceased to be a strange and alien institution divorced from the child's "other" life and family. There was, in the perceptual world of the child, a sudden falling into place, a relevancy to his entire school experience. There was also an elimination of much of the distrust and uncertainty among the parents about the middle-class institution known as "school."

Some plans for community involvement often are well-grounded and thoroughly researched before implementation. Others seem to emerge spontaneously and often disruptively out of frustration and need. One of these came about recently through some rather militant student action. Members of the Black Students' Union in a Los Angeles high school indicted what they described as racism in their 98 percent black school by demanding that the white principal be replaced. The distant and removed Board of Education got their hackles up (these were, after all, only students) and police were soon on the campus while student suspensions, some violence, and a boycott of classes went on. Finally, the black community, parents and local leaders, organized and made their demands known. Under the pressure of the constituency that rightfully represented the school population, the Board appointed a black principal (the man originally requested by the student group) and agreed to plans for negotiations between local parental committees and the principal on curricular and personnel matters. One wonders at the intractability of many of our institutional representatives; often harsh tensions need to exist before flexibility in standard operating procedures can be considered.

Meanwhile, there are cities where officials are attempting to anticipate the societal mood and to move creatively toward change rather than as a response to militant demand. Berkeley is, of course, one. Riverside, California, a semirural community, is another. And Philadelphia is a city which for a couple of years has been laying the groundwork for community participation and bureaucratic decentralization; in-service training sessions for teachers and administrators have marked their beginning. Other cities moving in this direction with some success are Detroit (where there are three times as many Negro administrators as in New York, although the school district is one-fourth the size), Chicago, Washington, and Baltimore.

New York provides an example of well-intentioned motivation with inadequate communication and planning. Decentralization and local involvement in that giant of a city were implemented without checkbacks and without the intense human communication that clearly was needed. The American Federation of Teachers strike there in 1968, in response to what they believed to be arbitrary local autocracy, caused deep wounds in the relationship between a relatively progressive union group and the black community. Such wounds are still unhealed, among many accusations of racism and counterracism.

The entire element of community participation in public education can also be thought of in terms of the power it affords to the powerless and the ultimate pride it gives to people who have never even comprehended the school bureaucracy, let alone influenced it. Perhaps the clearest and most tragic example of how the system of central control and its cultural exclusivity have incapacitated poor and different Americans is with the Indians of the Southwest.

The Bureau of Indian Affairs' schools are equipped to accept children at the age of six or seven (in early 1969, over 9000 under the age of nine were so placed). This means that they are taken from their parents, often several hundred miles. Weekend visits are difficult because of transportation intricacies, and are in fact tacitly discouraged by the Bureau because of the upsetting effect it has on the children. Parents not only do not see their young children, but are totally unaware of what is done to them in the schools—which may be a mercy.

In most instances the schools are housed in crumbling, even condemned shelters. The newer structures are aesthetically barren and functionally sterile—reinforcing a kind of military regimentation. Teachers are numbed by failure and quickly lose their spark and initiative. Counselors are rare. Curriculum is dictatorial (*only* English is permitted) and is directed away from anything to do with the Indian culture. A dehumanizing impact pervades the Bureau schools: Schedules for each child are posted in the dorms; each hour of each day is planned, and the schedules never vary; head counts occur regularly because some children run away; demerits are given for breaking rules; boys and girls are separated, and their fraternization is not encouraged; the suicide rate among young Indians in the boarding schools is over three times the national average. Only 16 percent of the Bureau's teachers are Indian, with little chance of any significant increase. (6)

It is painfully clear why Indians lack enthusiasm for anything connected with schools, education, book-learning, and the trappings of the Anglo world.

By contrast, at the Rough Rock Demonstration School in Northeastern Arizona (funded jointly by the BIA and the Office of Economic Opportunity), the entire Navaho boarding school is run by Indians. Included in the school's offerings are classes in Navaho language, history, and culture. There are ten counselors; parents are invited to live in the dorms for eight-week periods, are paid to work as dorm aides, and attend adult education classes; students are encouraged to go home on weekends and the school helps with the transportation; teachers visit the children's homes regularly to report on how they are doing. The school has included its community—the community has come into the school.

A recent report on the Rough Rock School closed with these words: "What the Indians at Rough Rock have proved is that given effective control of the immediate forces that shape their lives, they can be a success, [although] qualified in measurable achievement, total in terms of self-respect." (6)

What commands the compassion of all good people is the stark and ugly contrast between what might be and what is. What keeps coming back like an old refrain is the notion that a people gain dignity, pride, direction, and fulfillment from having meaningful control over their own destinies—from having, in a word, power.

What, then, are the specific ways within each classroom that diverse peoples can find relevancy? As the political naiveté of powerless people fades, and as they take significant action to influence their situation, it becomes imperative that they seek a curriculum (which all of us might seek) that has an intrinsic relationship to the lives they will lead. Such a curriculum is not plotted in any textbook. The writing which follows will not diagram it—it cannot if it is to respect its single indispensable characteristic: flexibility.

Notes

1. Charnofsky, Harold. "The Major League Professional Baseball Player: A Sociological Study." Unpublished doctoral dissertation, University of Southern California, 1968.

2. De Carava, Roy, and Langston Hughes. *The Sweet Flypaper of Life*. New York: Simon and Schuster, 1955.

3. Fanon, Frantz. *The Wretched of the Earth*. New York: Grove Press, 1968.

4. Guzman, Ralph. "The Gentle Revolutionaries," *West Magazine,* Los Angeles Times, January 26, 1969. Reprinted by permission of the author.

5. Halpern, Ray. "Tactics for Integration," *Saturday Review,* December 21, 1968, p. 48. Copyright 1968 Saturday Review, Inc. Reprinted by permission.

6. Henninger, Daniel, and Nancy Esposito. "Indian Schools—Regimented Non-Education." *The New Republic*. February 15, 1969, pp. 18–21.

7. King, Martin Luther, Jr. "The Role of the Behavioral Scientist in the Civil Rights Movement," *The American Psychologist,* March 1968.

8. Kozol, Jonathan. *Death at an Early Age*. Boston: Houghton Mifflin, 1967.

Chapter Six

A Relevant Curriculum

I Taught Them All

I have taught in high school for over 10 years. During that time I have given assignments, among others, to a murderer, an evangelist, a pugilist, a thief and an imbecile.

The murderer was a quiet little boy who sat on the front seat and regarded me with pale blue eyes; the evangelist, easily the most popular boy in the school, had the lead in the Junior play; the pugilist lounged by the window and let loose at intervals a raucous laugh that startled even the geraniums; the thief was a gay-hearted Lothario with a song on his lips; the imbecile a soft eyed little animal seeking the shadows.

The murderer awaits death in the state penitentiary; the evangelist has lain a year now in the village church-yard; the pugilist lost an eye in a brawl

in Hong Kong; the thief, by
standing on tiptoe, can see the windows
of my room from the county jail;
and the once gentle-eyed little moron
beats his head against a padded wall in
the state asylum.

    All of these pupils once sat in my
room, sat and looked at me gravely
across worn brown desks. I must have
been a great help to those pupils—
I taught them the rhyming scheme of
the Elizabethan sonnet and how to
diagram a complex sentence.

Anonymous, The Clearing House,
Farleigh Dickenson University, Teaneck,
New Jersey, November, 1937.
Reprinted by permission.

The purpose of a public education has become increasingly confused as the world becomes more technological and teachers more specialized. Radical college students deplore the so-called "indoctrination into the military-industrial complex" which they feel has become the university's primary function. Indeed, there is mounting evidence that many departments of our institutions of higher education have narrowed their focus to almost a single function: preparing students for economic homeostasis.

If such a situation does in fact exist, we have as a culture placed much distance between where we now are and where, according to the Spanish philosopher Jose Ortega y Gasset, we ought to be. Ortega, in his book *Mission of the University,* told us many years ago that the purpose of a college education was to bring its students to the *height of their times.* (14) Presumably that meant morally, spiritually, and aesthetically, as well as technically.

Our public schools tend to be ensnared in the same kind of single-purpose web that has surrounded our colleges; their philosophy, too, is that one needs to learn all he can so that he can become economically competitive in American society. But making economic success the *sine qua non* of education promulgates all sorts of distortions about the basic nature of human beings. Under such a schema, our children grow up deemphasizing human values and emphasizing economic ones. And then those minorities in our culture who do not observe such a hierarchy of values fail to achieve and fail to obtain even a modicum of economic stability. The system of education, because of its emphases, has a built-in bias against nonaggressive, noncompetitive, noneconomically saturated life styles.

Without being too grandiose, we might conjecture that our school curricula may be the primary villain in our society's failure to accept cultural diversity as a way of life.

Jerome Bruner (2) has told us, much later than Ortega, that the purpose of an education is to assist students to leap the barrier between learning and thinking. Thinking! Learning is only useful as it is transformed into the process of thinking.

What is a curriculum, then? What makes a curriculum relevant and meaningful? How can our schools accommodate all kinds of students and offer significant, tuned-in curricula to all of them? How can we —if we *have* slipped to a single-purpose curriculum—again broaden our base to permit the development and maturation of all kinds of goals among our students? How can we create and enhance the most human of scientists, plumbers, engineers, lawyers, carpenters, taxi drivers, doctors; and the most enlightened teachers, musicians, policemen, artists, secretaries, housewives?

Teaching No!
Learning Si!

Carl Rogers, the renowned American psychologist, in a paper now widely read in classes in teacher education, once shocked a teachers' conference at Harvard when he said that "anything that can be taught to another is relatively inconsequential." (15) He went on to state that anything really important could not be directly transmitted from person to person—that really significant learning had to be self-appropriated, reached out for and taken, as it were, by the learner.

Such a position is reminiscent of the old axiom which circulated through teacher-training circles a generation ago, that "more is caught than is taught." But when one suggests to young teachers or student teachers that the "hard sell" is relatively ineffective, that children learn by being excited about something, the response is inevitably phrased in terms of practicality. That is, schools have tremendous numbers of students, order must be maintained if anything is to be learned, and idealism is okay for the college course but not out on the job.

There is a kind of naive (and certainly conditioned) optimism that regardless of what organizational structure is placed upon students, they will ultimately come out stuffed with knowledge, endowed with wisdom, and convinced of the infinite superiority of the democratic approach. There is also a tacit assumption that the process of sending out information is identical to learning.

Actually, a "teacher" may send out all day long, but unless someone is receiving, no learning occurs. *Learning is the process of receiving stimuli, operating on those stimuli within a perceptual-conceptual framework, and accommodating the acquisition into some kind of active behavior.* Certainly something or someone *is* sending in order for the learner to be receiving. The structure of the sending is what has come to be known as teaching, and in a more refined sense can be called "curriculum."

In reality, the teacher (the sender or the structurer of stimuli) *is* the curriculum. As cited earlier in the Rosenthal research, (16) children tend to live up to expectations held for them. Nuances of teacher style and behavior influence the child's self-concept, motivation, and achievement. What more powerful curriculum is there, then, than the personal charisma of each teacher?

If this is so, then it might follow that a proper curriculum for youngsters who have little power and who have been nurtured in cultural diversity, is an enlightened, dynamic, receptive teacher. But it is not that simple.

Every individual operates on information within his unique perceptual framework. Therefore, what is important information to one person may, because of numerous experiences and ways of perceiving the world, be trivial to another. Then, the harder the "teacher" tries to communicate such information (sold as he is on its importance from his viewpoint) the more alienated or turned off the student becomes. Thus, some sensitive teachers will explain things four different ways in hopes that something in their world of experience could somehow speak to something in their students' worlds of experience. A *relevant curriculum* is one that says something to the perceptual world of the individual student. And so one aspect of the teacher-as-curriculum that needs to be explored is that of his flexibility as a human being to comprehend the perceptual differences in his children. Teaching should implement an environment which will allow children to, as it were, feast at the table. It is indeed the teacher who is the curriculum, but it is his expertise in ordering the learning environment that becomes an extension of himself and that ultimately becomes known as the classroom curriculum.

Some children, sadly, cannot feast at the table with the same gusto as others. Some have such impaired self-concepts that an open choice of nourishment offers only fear and apprehension. Have they drunk the poison of alienation so long that their health cannot be restored? Or are they weary travelers, dry from the journey, yes, but agonizing to soak up learning like the water from a long-elusive and finally found oasis? How are we to work in our schools with such divergent youngsters? Does their inadequacy (regardless of its cause) suggest that they need more control, more structure, more direction—or less? The implications in these questions are critical and need to be explored; this exploration will take two forms, a look at the existing situation, and a projection into a curriculum that might be.

The Curriculum the Way It Is

Several decades ago, a "progressive" curriculum was developed, which has now become standard around the country. It was known at first as *ability grouping,* but after much research by Guilford, (9) Thelen, (18) Getzels and Jackson, (7) and others into the nature of intelligence and its sometimes irregular endowment within any one individual, such organization is now called *tracking.* Youngsters in such systems may be in Track One (the highest) in math, but in Track Two (the middle) in English. Thus each child's strengths are recognized, and he is homogeneously grouped with others of similar strengths. Cape Kennedy, Florida, where the parents of many youngsters are scientists, was one of the early school districts to experiment with subject-matter tracking and with a nongraded secondary school. Theoretically, teachers have a smaller range of ability to contend with, and so children can progress much more quickly.

While certain aspects of the programs are laudable, such structuring leads to inequality. Developments such as nongraded and team-taught schools tend to increase individualization and respect for each student. But tracking, or ability grouping, tends also to send messages which help to degrade and to type many students.

It hardly takes expertise to perceive the critical emphasis in schools structured along lines of intellectual compatability. *Virtually all other elements of human growth in education are at once subservient to the trait of technical aptitude.* There is no doubt that the blasting off of Sputnik in 1957 gave impetus to the already accelerating swing toward technical training as the primary goal of public education. Social awareness (including the acceptance of cultural diversity) became suspect as a legitimate concern of schools. Reactionary forces in education took the ascendency and began to weed out what they called frills and social-living courses. Ability grouping and track systems logically provided the best arrangement to sustain the pure pursuit of knowledge.

Curriculum became, and still is, something imposed by an external decision upon a given child or classroom. (This is hardly appropriate within the context of the earlier discussion that children have unique perceptual worlds and will appropriate what is meaningful to them.)

Of course, the organizational pattern in any given school is not, of itself, the curriculum. But in fact the group in which a student is placed and the expectations held for him become powerful elements in his learning pattern.

The track system fits neatly into the middle-class American system of exclusivity. It sets up *desiderata* and then ensures the success of all who fit the mold. Powerless American children of minority cultural backgrounds, having a much less technical emphasis in their life styles, usually find themselves on Track Three. In schools where letters substitute for numbers, they are in the Z group. Of course, at the elementary level reading groups are formed and labeled "bluebirds, sparrows, and robins"; but everyone in class knows which one is a euphemism for Track Three. The human degradation—the self-fulfilling lowering of expectations—begins its insidious work, and the track system is its tool.

Today, we teach as a standard procedure: that Columbus discovered America; that our Constitution was written by inspired, freedom-loving men; that the Indians were wild savages or primitives and merely nameless villains who tried to scalp all whites; that slaves were happy and sang in their bondage; that our nation has always kept its treaties. From the perspective of the emerging minorities in America: vast Indian cultures beat Columbus to it, and in Central and South America they had developed extremely sophisticated societies; our founding fathers were right in their principles, but in reality they were slaveholders; our Indians were only "primitive" in the sense that they were a familial people, wedded to the earth and to nature, dependent upon the land and the animals for their survival, and not surprisingly resistant to annihilation; * our slave-era was perhaps the most shameful time in the world's history—blacks were used and bred like animals and were far from happy, as their music and writings show; the Treaty of Guadalupe Hidalgo was supposed to guarantee the Mexican in America, who had just been absorbed by our country when the great Southwest was annexed, freedom to continue his language, his culture, his way of life—this treaty has been ignored.

At least from some perspectives, the latter series is the way it *really* was as America developed; the former series is the way it has been told in our schools, as the curriculum is today.

The way it is today, the schools will not admit that the entire environment in and around each school becomes the overpowering curriculum of that school. In middle-class neighborhoods, the environ-

---

* A whimsical anecdote seems appropriate here. Benjamin Franklin (in his *Wit and Folly*) once attacked the notion of Indians as savages.

"*Savages we call them,* because their manners differ from ours, which we think the Perfection of Civility; they think the same of theirs. . . ."

He then describes an incident at the Treaty of Lancaster, in Pennsylvania, in 1744, between the Six Nations and the Government of Virginia.

"After the principal Business was settled, the Commissioners from Virginia acquainted the Indians by a Speech, that there was at Williamsburg a College with a Fund for Educating Indian Youth, and that if the Chiefs of the Six Nations would send down half a Dozen of their Sons to that College, the Government would take Care that they should be well provided for, and instructed in all the Learning of the White People. It is one of the Indian Rules of Politeness not to answer a public Proposition the same day that it is made; they think it would be treating it as a light Matter; and that they show it Respect by taking time to consider it, as of a Matter important. They therefore deferred their Answer till the day following; when their Speaker began by expressing their deep Sense of the Kindness of the Virginia Government, in making them that Offer; for we Know, says he, that you highly esteem the kind of Learning taught in those Colleges, and that the Maintenance of our Young Men while with you, would be very expensive to you. We are convinced therefore that you mean to do us good by your Proposal, and we thank you heartily. But you who are wise must know, that different Nations have different Conceptions of things; and you will therefore not take it amiss, if our Ideas of this Kind of Education happen not to be the same with yours. We have had some Experience of it. Several of our Young People were formerly brought up at the Colleges of the Northern Provinces; they were instructed in all your Sciences; but when they came back to us, they were bad Runners, ignorant of every means of living in the Woods, unable to bear either Cold or Hunger, Knew neither how to build a Cabin, take a Deer, or Kill an Enemy, spoke our Language imperfectly; were therefore neither fit for Hunters, Warriors, or Counsellors; they were totally good for nothing. We are however not the less obliged by your kind Offer, tho' we decline accepting it; and to show our grateful Sense of it, if the Gentlemen of Virginia will send us a dozen of their Sons, we will take great Care of their Education, instruct them in all we Know, and make *Men* of them."

ment reinforces the classroom didactics, and most children feel relatively unthreatened (if unmotivated). In poverty neighborhoods, the environment belies the instruction, which says all men are created equal—the segregated and unequal schools belie that. The instruction says all men have a chance in the land of the free—the unemployed on the corner defy that. The instruction says that America is a melting pot—the instructor, his administrators, the counselors, their remarkable cultural sameness refute that. And the *subtlety* of some of the environmental curricula is often particularly pernicious. Consider the following anecdote:

The principal of an urban high school with a population that was 70 percent Mexican-American took great pride in publicizing the neatness and cleanliness of his campus. In addition, he regularly announced publicly how well-behaved his students were, how there were seldom fights, very little pilfering, virtually no smoking on campus, and that his students all looked neat and well-groomed. Privately, to his teachers, he would confess that the school had to emphasize making these students good, respectable citizens, since most would not go far academically. The average from each graduating class who went on to college was in the range of 10 to 15 percent. Thirty-five percent did not finish high school.

What the principal never explained was that the campus was clean because he had ordered trash cans for virtually every nook and corner (one could close his eyes, toss a banana peel in the air, and be fairly sure it would land in a container); teachers on yard duty stumbled on the cans regularly. There were seldom fights, because a campus edict expelled all fighters regardless of fault or explanation. Stealing and smoking were given second chances, but expulsion was the order for a second offense. Codes of dress and grooming were so stringent that long hair, balloon pants, pegged pants, slacks for girls, mustaches, sideburns, sandals, etc., were outlawed.

The overall effect was a kind of a deflating of the ego of every youngster in the school. Of course they would not achieve academically! They were not expected to—nor was their school environment structured to encourage them. There was a singular lack of curiosity evident in the students. The campus had the smell of intellectual death about it, the smothered aroma of old furniture covered with dusty sheets.

That principal, a year or two later, went onward and upward into the superintendent's office—a reward for his sterling handling of a tricky position. But there are currently signs that the youth are restless. Fights have occurred lately at that school. Pickets have marched. Parents have visited the School Board. Change could be in the air— but not as a result of any initiative on the part of the school or the system. And until change does come, that is still the way it is at that high school; the school *is* the curriculum.*

Most of the works published in the last few years dealing with education for diverse people are saturated with the notion (not necessarily conscious) that diversity itself is a disadvantage. The books and periodicals are replete with remedies for redressing the grievances of the disadvantaged—many of them geared toward institutional adjustment and accommodation. This focus should tell us that our educational structures have not been tooled up to cope with diversity.

Further, however, these writings, perhaps more through their titles than their content, (4,5,19) continue to instruct young teachers that many of our Americans come into our schools riveted to a kind of sordid underculture; that our youngsters are handicapped or disadvantaged because they are culturally deprived. Perhaps the Rosenthal phenomenon, the self-fulfilling attitude, operates at this level as well.

It is not our function to perpetuate cultural exclusivity by labeling our beautifully diverse youngsters as "disadvantaged." But the way it is today, our curriculum is composed of rules which further conformity and castigate divergence. One junior high school in California, rather typical of many, distributes the sheet reproduced as Figure 1 to all incoming seventh graders.

It must be mentioned that the school which operates on these standards includes about one-third Mexican-American children and one-third Negro children. Consider VIII of Figure 1 and imagine expecting such a thing of a Mexican-American youngster with 11 brothers and sisters living in a three-room house—his sense of negative difference is at once apparent to him. In fact, consider the entire list in the context of a positive and constructive guide for youngsters of varying degrees of self-confidence and personal power; virtually every sentence carries with it a tone of admonition, whether it is positively or negatively phrased. Only item A of X can be construed as neutral and helpful to all children who might be entering the school.

The way it is now, except in experimental schools, the in-classroom structure is generalized (as opposed to individualized) and is geared to the class average. The brighter child who finishes early finds boredom if he conforms and castigation if he digresses. The slower child, or the unacculturated child, finds little relevance and is often ignored. The general curriculum guide for each grade level comes

---

* It is desirable, among members of the powerful, not to admit to institutional deficiency. For years, our school spokesmen have indicted the students and ignored the schools in explaining failure among the powerless. As a former Chairman of the Boston School Committee proclaimed just a few years ago, "We have no inferior education in our schools. What we have been getting is an inferior type of student."

Figure 1. The school is the curriculum.

Junior High Student Code

The following code must be observed by everyone if it is to be really effective in helping our school become better and make each of us proud of our school, and our school proud of us.

I. In assemblies we:
   A. Respect the flag and our National Anthem.
   B. Enter the auditorium quickly and quietly.
   C. Take our seats promptly.
   D. Are courteous by showing our appreciation for the performance.
   E. Leave the auditorium only when told to do so, and then in an orderly manner.

II. On the campus we:
   A. Help to keep the campus clean.
   B. Eat only in the lunch area.
   C. Do not play or run in the lunch area.

III. In the classroom we:
   A. Prepare for work before the tardy bell rings.
   B. Are quiet and pay attention.
   C. Respect the ideas and opinions of both teachers and pupils.
   D. Stand or speak only when called on to speak.
   E. Do not mark on or deface school property, and we realize that it is our responsibility to care for materials and books checked out to us.
   F. Are a credit to our regular teacher, our school, and ourselves by cooperating with substitute teachers.
   G. Leave in an orderly way.

IV. To have good citizenship we:
   A. Accept our responsibility by obeying rules made for the safety and good of others.
   B. Try to be cheerful and understanding to all.
   C. Appreciate what we are learning and try to improve every group and class to which we belong.

V. In the halls we:
   A. Never run, push or shove.
   B. Stay on the right side.
   C. Never eat.

VI. To be good leaders we:
   A. Demonstrate honesty.
   B. Cooperate with students and teachers.
   C. Take criticism well without resentment.
   D. Set a good example for others to follow.

    E. Guide ourselves and our friends toward a definite goal.

VII. On the field we:
    A. Display good sportsmanship at all times.
    B. Always use athletic equipment safely and carefully.
    C. Always accept the decision of the referee.
    D. Never use bad language.

VIII. At home we:
    A. Have a desk or table at which to study.
    B. Keep our books and study materials in one place.
    C. Have a definite time set aside for study.
    D. Have a well-lighted place away from television and other distractions where we can study.

IX. Our locker:
    A. Combination is not to be given to any other pupil, not even our best friend.
    B. Is not to be shared unless our homeroom teacher tells us to do so.
    C. Is to be kept neat and orderly at all times.

X. Our school library:
    A. Is open before school, at brunch, at lunch and after school.
    B. Has books which may be checked out but which are to be returned on the date due.
    C. Is a place for quiet individual reading and study.

---

from the mysterious and awesome downtown office, and it instructs the teachers in all the expectations for all the children in any given grade. It is much like Gesell's book on child rearing (6), which was based on a developmental model of human growth and which guided thousands of American mothers toward the expected behavior of their children at any given chronological point.

Some strict developmental theories still influence, and in many cases govern, our school curricula despite ongoing evidence that environmental stimuli can radically distort any normative types of behavior patterns. Our schools, in short, are structured on an expectation program—that children, on the average, will learn certain things at a certain age. And our instruction is calibrated to fit the so-called average student—who does not really exist.

Reading is, of course, taught on that basis. All children engage in pre-primer work simultaneously and are expected to begin to learn to read at the age of six. Those who do not learn are sent to a designated table to await personalized drill. The damage done to many of the bright but unready youngsters when they are blatantly made aware of their deficiency is a crime. Some never recover, and study remedial reading throughout their elementary school days—even though the standardized tests they take somehow show them to have average or better intelligence. Experience by now surely should have taught us that children if stimulated and excited will reach for ideas and skills; these same children if frustrated will wilt and withdraw. ("What happens to a dream deferred? Does it dry up like a raisin in the sun?" (11))

The way it is today, children are routinely admonished to "speak good English!" Those who speak street language, farm language, mountain language, or language with a Spanish accent are made to feel not only stupid but ashamed of themselves. Some schools drill endlessly on grammar; sentences are still diagrammed, out of context with any student writings; pronunciation is not only corrected, but the teacher will sometimes use a group chorus to set the child straight. How humiliating! (One professor from a western university, with tongue in cheek, recently pointed out that what Spanish-speaking, Chicano children really needed was the chance to learn key phrases in English that would be useful to them in their daily encounters with the American world—phrases such as "Pay me," "Don't push me," "I want a raise," "Pick your own damned grapes.")

At the other extreme, and without tongue in cheek, a high school principal was heard to ask of a college opportunities program, "I hope you can teach all these kids to speak English without an accent. You know you can tell 'em right off on the phone by the way they talk. And they will never be able to get good jobs." One wonders if he realized what he was saying about our middle-class culture.

Today our teachers and administrators (indeed our society) address culturally diverse youngsters and their families as "you people," "you," "your people." School personnel speak of "them," "these children," "those parents," "theirs." A linguistic chasm becomes an audible representation of the cultural chasm that exists between the schools and the people.

While our middle-class students can be cajoled or bribed into learning or memorizing dead or irrelevant material (the threat of grades, parental collusion, the conditioned value that gratification should be deferred and hard work makes one good), most of the culturally different cannot be pressured this way. Consider, for example, our insistence that everyone learn the dates of the signing of the Articles of Confederation, the Battle of Gettysburg, the start of World War I; or our preoccupation with honor students, scholarship winners, athletic successes, talented musicians; or the *ways* we attempt to "teach" our youngsters; books, recitations, written essays, blackboard work. More relevant would be a comparison between America's original attempts at setting up codes of law and at demanding her rights, with the "ten demands of the Black Students' Union" at the nearby college; or a comparison between the Boston Tea Party (an act of civil disobedience) and the Montgomery, Alabama, sit-in; or a drawing of a parallel between student demands for reform and participation at San Francisco State College in 1968, with the drives for self-government at a hundred different points in American history. More relevant would be the use of recognition for many diverse skills, most of them much more practical to the real-life world of our center-city students than the remnants of past-day talents we continue to exalt. More relevant would be the use of more exciting and intimate and humanizing methods of communication than we use now—such as touching, seeing, manipulating, interacting, role-playing, pantomime, field trips, anecdotes, experiments.

A final anecdote should serve to characterize our schools' current curricular mediocrity, especially as it is applied to the poor and the different. A young substitute teacher recently described her experience in a virtually all-black elementary school in a large urban center. She was substituting for a teacher in a social adjustment class (problem cases) for fifth and sixth grade children. The class was small, and the children were all boys. Hoping to begin with a positive approach (she was cautioned by, of all people, the school clerk, that it would be a miserable day for her and she should call the office if she needed help), she began to move the heavy tables out of the way so she could put the chairs in a small circle and sit with the boys. They acted willing to help her but registered astonishment and apprehension at her moving the tables. "See them red circles?" one of them said, "Well, that's where the legs of them tables s'posed to go. We ain't allowed to move them." The teacher told them she would put them back before the day was over and that their regular teacher would never know.

She sat and talked with the boys for 30 minutes, making no demands, asking them about themselves. She had observed several of the boys running in the yard before class and made a mental note to cash in on what seemed to be a real strength, later in the afternoon, when they were getting restless.

She had bought some comic books on the way to the school that morning and had brought with her a set of plastic Constructo-Straws. The boys noticed the straws and asked about them. She passed them out, and a short while later all the children were engrossed in a common construction project. Later they read the comic books. They volunteered to clean up before lunch; one boy fastidiously washed all the brushes after the children had done some painting. (The boys were amazed that they could paint, saying that they never painted in that teacher's class.)

The boys said that they enjoyed singing, and they had never heard their voices recorded before, so the teacher told them she would get a tape recorder from the office and they could record their voices. She asked the vice-principal on two occasions to have the tape recorder brought to the room, but it never did get there.

Later, when they raced, the teacher used a stopwatch, but only showed the time to the boy who recorded it—the boys were reluctant to take a chance on the winner-loser situation. (They had never raced against time before; nor had their teacher ever taken an interest in their running.)

At one point in the day, the boys expressed fear that their regular teacher would really be "hoppin' " if they didn't do *some* of the regular schoolwork. So they began to do some textbook and workbook drills. *At no point in the day was there any serious social disturbance.*

Just before the close of school, the teacher encouraged the boys to sing out, if they wanted to, even without the recorder. Some did, and although they were self-conscious about it, seemed to show genuine pleasure in the activity.

When the final bell rang, the children did not leave. They lingered around the room, talking to the teacher, helping her clean up. They asked her if she could come back the next day. They asked her if she could be their regular teacher. (Their regular teacher was about to become a Vice Principal—this social-adjustment experience had been his exposure to "special" education.)

After the children did finally leave, the teacher looked through their anecdotal folders. The boy who helped clean the paint brushes had a history of getting down on the floor on all fours and howling like a dog. Another boy was considered a bully and a latent sociopath. Had she read the records before the class, her approach might have been affected; as it was, she was positively dumbfounded at the contrast between what had occurred and what the folders showed. Teachers from adjoining rooms were literally astounded by the serenity of her day.

As she left the school, when the clerk saluted her with, "I am sure you will have a better day tomorrow, wherever you are," she replied, "I had a perfectly lovely day today!"

A Curriculum that Might Be

In the middle 1950s, educators were debating the merits of a logical versus a psychological curriculum. The logical was based upon research into developmental and learning theory and subsumed certain stages of readiness in learning. The classroom approach would be geared to the logical (from the teacher's or the curriculum co-ordinator's perspective) and the sequential presentation of subject matter. The psychological curriculum grew out of earlier theories of John Dewey and other pragmatists who reasoned that children learn when they are personally and psychologically ready. The classroom organization, then, could not be imposed externally, nor could any approach indeed be considered logical for any given student if it were spawned by someone else.

The psychological approach to the organization of learning—the notion that each person orders his environmental stimuli in a unique and individually sequential way—has had its ups and downs. The ideas of Rogers, cited earlier, dovetail neatly into this psychological model; one can only teach from his own personal perspective, and one learns from a different one.

By these definitions, our examination of a truly useful and relevant curriculum has its foundation in a psychological rather than a logical orientation. With this in mind, some specifics can be tentatively explored. They are obviously not exhaustive, but are samples from the vast panorama of ways in which children of diversity can benefit from having facets of their school curriculum structured.

Since the standard means of passing on information ("teaching") in our schools has always focused upon the use of textbooks, we shall respond to expectation and begin by exploring the entire notion of textbooks and textbook learning. Perhaps we can show that books can be alive and meaningful and intrinsic and useful as curricular tools. Perhaps we can show that it does not have to be the way it has been with books. In so doing, perhaps we can dispell a suspicion that may have been aroused in the critical reader that my intent has been, in this book, to discredit the importance of cognition and incisive thinking. This has not been my intent. The fact is that cognitive activity and expression are best nurtured in a framework that is affectively alluring to the learner. Our standard textbooks, certainly suspect in their format as optimal learning aids for middle-class students, are downright abominations for the poor and the powerless.

Textbooks

It is odd how a given writing or research can make significant impact on our educational structure in the abstract, while in the concrete little, if any, change occurs. *Teacher,* (21) by Sylvia Ashton Warner, has been such a book. Miss Warner's notion of an "organic curriculum" which grows out of the creative energy of the learners has much to recommend it to our attempt to be meaningful to powerless students. Students write their own stories and learn to read their own words. Cognition *is* the order of the day, but it becomes active through highly personal and highly interesting subject matter.

There is mounting evidence that a personalized kind of reading experience can have distinct impact on learners unaccustomed to success in traditional school-type activities. One remarkable instance of this has been occurring at a mission school for young Papago Indian children.

At San Xavier Mission School, near Tuscon, Arizona, a forward-looking teacher (who had been exposed to a unique in-service summer institute on educating young Indian children) encouraged and assisted her students and their parents to create their own textbook. Children worked at writing and describing their own lives. Dozens of photographs were taken and the parents and children chose those which they believed were most representative of their condition to be the illustrations in the book. The title, too, was made personal: *Our Book.* (10) (See Figure 2.)

In a more urban setting, the central office of the Los Angeles City Schools sent out a call for people to write "high-interest, low-vocabulary" readers. The need was for readers for seventh and eighth graders (almost all minority youngsters) with third or fourth grade reading abilities. Several such books were written and are in use, (17,20) and the reaction initially appears to be fruitful. Youngsters find that the stories are about their lives and their activities (some have even recognized themselves in a given tale), and that they are readable. Textbooks usually tend to grow old and ragged and finally be discarded; but students have actually been walking off with these books, with the result that their number is rapidly diminishing. That in itself is some kind of tribute. But why shouldn't *all* our texts for those who are advanced in grade but arrears in skills be "high-interest, low-vocabulary" books?

Language and Projective Activities

Almost all the powerless youngsters in our schools have little experience with verbal abstractions. Their family interactions have often been dominated by the struggle for survival in a hostile world. Verbal communication, whether among transplanted ghetto blacks, encapsulated Spanish-speaking Puerto Ricans or "Chicanos," or rural whites, has been colloquial, to the point, perhaps unique in syntax and in phrasing, and certainly primarily concrete and oriented in the here and now. Our schools are saturated with complex verbal subtleties which escape the poor and thereby exclude them. We need to avoid endless verbal description, explanation, and rhetoric; our children must *do* rather than be told.

It would be tempting to latch on to any of the several gimmicks that have hit the market which attempt to put activity into learning. Most of these must be resisted. However, some game-type devices, produced after careful research, have shown in practice that they are

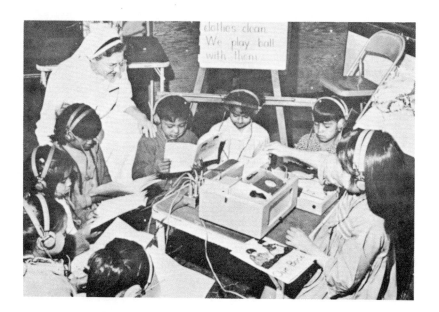

We like to use this machine.
It helps us with our reading and numbers. We learn to read.
We learn our numbers, too.
    Many of us talk Papago. We learn to read Papago.
This machine helps us.
    Some of us talk Spanish. We learn to read Spanish, too.
We like to use this machine.

Figure 2. *Our Book*. Page from a textbook created by
Papago students and parents.

Hubatch, Sister M. Antoninus, O.S.F. *Our Book,* San Xavier del Bac, Tucson, Arizona, 1968. Reprinted by permission.

useful for learners with impaired verbal motivation. Such games involve the learner physically, emotionally, and intellectually, and are often absorbing.

A complete format for encouraging reticent powerless children to use language has been published. It is called the Matrix Games. Their introductory booklet describes the games in this way:

Matrix Games are carefully sequenced sets of pictures and instructions to be used with groups of young children in order to give them systematic practice in language concepts. The lessons range from ten to twenty-five minute periods depending on the content of the Matrix and the attention span of the children. (8)

The games are geared to help children learn to follow directions (e.g., "First put a red X on the boy walking the dog, then put a blue circle on the man riding the horse."); thus a child hears two directions, must discriminate among shapes and colors, and find the two correct pictures among the 16 on the matrix. He must also get involved by taking some action. He hears, sees, and feels.

Children also give verbal accounts of what they have done, learning to speak clearly and more fluently. They learn to integrate certain complex cognitive abilities by sorting out common elements in some task. They learn independence by gradually assuming more responsibility for directing their own games. And they develop new vocabulary in a sequential manner, seeing and recognizing grouped concepts, such as in the Pet Matrix or in the Color Matrix.

In effect, the Matrix Games are programmed sequentially and are flexible enough to allow for individualized pacing and small group follow-up. One teacher, working in a Trenton, New Jersey, school, told me with great enthusiasm how her young children were being excited by and progressing in language development with the use of these games. And while certainly no panacea for all the problems confronting the culturally different and the verbally handicapped in our schools, Matrix Games represent one orderly way of providing high-interest language exposure.

Many examples could illustrate the specifics of developing the language of powerless students. But these would create a patchwork of "how-to's" and not a cohesive philosophy that a creative teacher must learn to apply. In general, the poor come to the urban schools speaking what amounts to a foreign language. It is foreign to the middle-class school authorities and it would be considered a mystery by most powerful, well-to-do Americans.

The task confronting the schools is how to enhance the communicative abilities of diverse youngsters without shaming them for what they are and can do. One way to do this is to approach the teaching of English to rurally conditioned youngsters as if it were a foreign language. Reports have circulated of schools attempting this with unusual success, especially in some Southern states. Children then feel quite adequate about knowing two languages: the one their family and their environment have nurtured in them, and the one expected of them at school. The degradation associated with "mistakes," which characterizes much of today's approach to language deviations, disappears. To do this, however, requires as much of an education for the teacher—his biases, his rigidity—as it does for the learner.

To teach English as a second language to diverse youngsters may be the key to relieving much of the dissidence now apparent in our schools. Secondary school youngsters, consistently thwarted from expressing themselves in the way their life experience has taught them, face critical identity problems. Their frustrations leave them hostile and truculent. Often they have already developed two languages, one for the street and one for the school, and have come to feel guilty for this achievement.

But support has recently grown for the thesis held by many linguists that "ghettoese" is a valid language in that those who speak it can communicate fluently with others who know that language. Such linguists corroborate the idea that English should then be taught to these students as a second or foreign language. (Although it should be noted that other educators, such as Kenneth B. Clark, have expressed firm opposition to the ghetto language approach, claiming that all learners must be held to the standard as established by the larger society.)

How a person is made to perceive himself as a communicator may indeed be a major factor in his total commitment to the pursuit of other abstractions or to his trust in the school system and his other potentials. . . .

An article in the *Saturday Review* in early 1969 (1) takes our schools to task for their neglect of the so-called "show" section of the curriculum. The "real" curriculum has been concerned with mastering subject matter, preparing for the proper job, etc. The "show" curriculum has been concerned with the human values an education can foster: good feelings, personal growth, sensitivity towards others. But very little is done about it.

The Human Objectives

With powerless children, human values cannot be reserved merely for show, because they are so much more on the surface with people of rural outlook. With middle-class Americans, at an early age emotions are thrust far behind a facade of language abstractions. With rural Americans, the feeling level—the level of nuances, of gestures, of body contact, of eye contact—lingers for many years. Black youngsters learn early that the white man's words do not always fit his actions, and so they become highly sensitized to nonverbal communication. Once, leaving a meeting where black students and white school administrators had concluded a sharp verbal and emotional exchange, I heard a black student complain that "the man was jivin' us," while I had perceived (focused as I was on his words) that he had told it straight. In fact, the student was later proven correct. As the lyrics of a recent recording tell us: "Y'all done made me have a radar mind; and even when I look into your eyes I can tell when you're lyin'." (12)

An "affective curriculum" seems particularly vital today when we consider that the world has the technical expertise to destroy its institutions but little social expertise in governing them. Such a curriculum would indeed be as much needed by powerful, middle-class children as by the powerless.

Children must be encouraged to express their feelings in open dialogue and activity. Aggressions must be allowed their expression, perhaps in physically guided ways: arm wrestling, pushing, or refereed yelling. Group encounter situations ought certainly to be explored as conscious ways of educating for social intimacy and awareness. College campuses are finding such groups valuable as aids in counselor education, teacher education, and just plain student-faculty interaction.

One effect of an emphasis on human objectives in our schools would be to bring closer together the feelings children have and their abilities to express them. Children often cannot communicate how they feel to their teacher or to their schoolmates. Misunderstanding is anathema to education. There can be no question about the teacher's need to "connect" with her students. As it is today, the awareness of one's feelings and the enhancement of human values are left up to chance in our schools. The way it might be, the curriculum could plan for such exposures.

Children as Teachers

We have discovered recently (with astonishment and some chagrin) that eight-year-olds can teach six-year-olds. But the model has been with us for some time. Alcoholics Anonymous, Synanon, therapy groups—all have been sending the message that people who are close to a situation, who have just gone through an experience, have an increased capacity to communicate with those currently going through it.

It is such a realization that has led to the recent emphasis on the use of paraprofessionals in community work. Indeed, several major colleges and universities have instituted degrees in applied or functional behavioral science—where a student will do a major share of his undergraduate work in an on-the-job urban setting. After four years or fewer he will be equipped to work as a helping agent without intense graduate study or the formerly required degrees and credentials.

That nonprofessionals with personal involvement can be of unusual help to others in need was most graphically illustrated to a colleague and myself in 1967. During a pilot counseling group to help parents cope with sons and daughters who had become too antisocial to remain in regular school settings, it was found that our professional training and stature were all but useless. The parents virtually ignored the group initiators and interacted with each other. Somehow, to know that others had had similar situations to confront, and to know how they had handled their problems, provided a therapy and an insight which the professionals could not duplicate.

Why our schools have become among the last to discover these relationships is a bit perplexing. No doubt the real or imagined threat to the status of the teacher has something to do with it. But the fact is with us: Eight-year-olds can and do teach six-year-olds.

They always have. It is just that we have become so engrossed in the technicalities and methodologies of the teaching process that we have forgotten the rudiments of the learning process. In classroom group discussion, children are asked to recite out loud so that all can share their solutions to the problem at hand. We are aware of this strategy; we plan for it. Why then do we not plan for individual tutoring between students?

In some forward-looking schools where individualized study programs are flourishing, it is most exciting to see children divided into pairs, one reading to the other, both huddled over their books, intent upon sharing the material and alert to each other's progress.

In other classrooms, fifth and sixth grade boys who themselves have been behavior problems to the teachers, have found renewed motivation in tutoring first and second grade boys. Usually the demonstrative older boy will gravitate to the demonstrative younger one, and a communion of a sort takes place. One situation emerges as kind of a classic. A usually-in-trouble fifth grade boy became the first person in the entire school to be able to get a withdrawn first grade boy to say a few words out loud.

Culturally different youngsters, poor youngsters, youngsters with impaired expectations, find their relationships with the professional teacher to be difficult and tense; with their culture-mates they find a harmony, a language style, a commonality of outlook. The ghetto child must have intimate contact with older children in his school. The benefit is two-way. The younger child sees a model, relates to a "brother," feels a relevancy to his activities. The older child experiences the helper's role, gains the confidence of his relative maturity, knows empathy, feels admiration and respect. It is known that a close human relationship between a helper and a learner enhances the learner's receptivity. It remains for our schools to make use of this knowledge.

Creativity

So much of our curriculum has been convergent in nature. Just as our system of grades and promotions is lock-step, so has our curriculum been synchronized and sterilized. We must encourage all our children to think creatively—and with powerless youngsters we must encourage it because it will lead to an assumption of power.

Powerless, degraded children wither and turn inward when a teacher spotlights them with a question requiring an imaginative response. This says more about the nature of powerlessness than it does about ethnic, racial, or cultural attributes. Lack of power breeds inhibition and stifles the freedom to be imaginative. By the time a child is in the third grade, his confidence wanes and he refuses to reach out. This is like negative feedback; when a subject reaches out but finds his hand slapped often enough, he becomes inhibited from venturing out again.

A creative curriculum is one which leads children into unique and imaginative structures. It is one which includes, from the start of school, opportunities for open-ended physical, intellectual, and artistic activities. Children must be encouraged to engage in whatever unique activities *their* culture performs. Indian children can, for example, be encouraged to find gourds, to paint them, to play ball with them, to make maracas with them. Mexican-American students can be encouraged to construct and paint piñatas, in any form and in any design that their imaginations can conceive. Music, dance, word games, stories, role-playing, pictures, ceramic work, finger-painting, sand-painting, construction materials—all provide outlet and expression in diverse forms.

One resourceful Anglo teacher provided her fourth grade, largely Mexican-American class with an opportunity to do more than study about the California missions. The children (with the help of a father or two) actually built the pitched roof and columns of a mission at one end of the classroom. The project required measuring, drawing, cutting, hammering, painting, trimming, and even reading. The creativity of the children was remarkable, and their energy was released in motivated, purposeful, imaginative activity.

In classrooms where there are many powerless children, an allowance for divergent thinking would encourage the process of abstracting. Inhibited students are unskilled in abstract thinking; they have little experience with semantic and ideational subtleties. Their inhibitions about *themselves* make them inhibited about their *ideas,* and they are afraid to express them.

A creative classroom structure specially geared to uplift powerless, inhibited youngsters, would be one with few top-heavy sanctions and with many open-ended choices. When children begin to make choices and see that they are not rejected—that their ideas are really okay— they become more willing to try. A curriculum which grows out of the students' willingness to try *becomes* relevant.

One black teacher enrolled in a summer National Defense Education Act institute, in 1966, in her last-day speech to the entire group, addressed herself to much of what has been said above. Her colleagues were deeply touched by the emotion and the philosophy which had been stirred in her through her in-service experience. Some of her words are presented here:

We need some new goals (in education). We need to move from: a preoccupation with order and neatness; a preoccupation with knowing rather than going; a preoccupation with cookbook approaches; a preoccupation with the notion that only adult concepts are good; a preoccupation with whatever produces force and coercion; a preoccupation with grading and grades, with lock-step organization, with the notion that mistakes are sinful.

People who are afraid to make mistakes will not try. If we are going to have people who are afraid to make mistakes we are not going to have very bright people.

We need to move to whatever enhances the self-concept, whatever opens up the child's experience. We must teach children that the world is something to confront and not something to evade.

The individual self must be valued. We must provide children with wide choices. There must be trust and respect for the student. We must encourage more cooperative learning, for more learning takes place cooperatively. Differences must be valued, for differences are the essence of creativity. We must create a feeling that anything is worth examining. We must have more tolerance for noise and confusion. We must be more positive in our criticism. We must value spontaneity. . . . No child is hopeless. There is something we can do for every child . . . man will become the best of what he can be, when you and I have set him free. . . . (3)

This thoughtful teacher has stirred many other teachers, young student teachers, teachers-in-training, through the publicizing and the promulgation of her insights. But such insights need practical outlets. Creativity and relevancy and curiosity, as stated earlier, are deeply involved with the character and the personality of the teacher, the facilitator. And yet, there are some structures and materials which can contribute, in a very practical way, to creative classroom approaches.

Again, to be helpful but not tedious, one example will be given of a publication which offers opportunity for imaginative and personalized expression. It appeared in California in 1968, and is called the *No War Toys Book for Young Writers and Illustrators*. (13) It is a notebook divided into two parts. The first half of the book is composed solely of illustrations done by young children. The page opposite each illustration is blank and provides space for children to create a story about the picture they see. The second half of the book is composed of a sentence or a word on each page. The opposite page is left blank so that children can create a picture about the word(s) they have read. (See Figure 3.)

Whatever half the child starts with, the finished product is a book half-written and half-illustrated by the child himself. The kinds of creative and intellectual activity this structure affords need not be belabored. Children whom I have observed using this book have seemed gleeful about the activity, and have prized their finished work as well.

Divergent thinking need not be a product of chance; it could be made a necessary ingredient in the enhancing of a child's expressive ability.

*Educational
Media*

We started this examination of a relevant curriculum with a discussion of the standard classroom tool for learning, the textbook. Now, a brief discussion of newer and more elastic modes of communication seems in order.

We commonly think of educational media as requiring literacy, since books and the reading and writing skills have always been central in teaching-learning strategies. Some media do not require literacy, and these seem rather appropriate for use with culturally different students. They include tape recordings, disc recordings, language laboratories, television, motion pictures, film strips, etc.

These media carry several sensory modalities. The most frequently used are seeing and hearing, but the senses of touch (such as in speech-correction work and other language approaches) and of smell and taste (such as in laboratory experiences, nutrition, health) can be integrated into the primary media modes. Children with impaired reading or writing can begin to find some success and achievement through viewing, listening, touching, and actively engaging all their senses.

Imaginative teachers have begun to look for ways of providing students with the use of certain media that can be enhancing for them. I recall one twelfth grade teacher who recognized the usefulness of multisensory investigations, when he announced his acceptance of any medium of reporting as fulfilling the requirements of a term project in his Contemporary American Problems class. Two youths teamed in filming the pivot at second base, performed by a professional baseball player, a college player, and a high school player. Their aim was to analyze the expertise of one player over the others, and to discover, if possible, the footwork or body movements that went into successful second base performance. A girl in the class tape-recorded and edited a debate she attended at the local Youth Opportunities Center, where an integrationist and a segregationist went at it. She combined her presentation to the class with her own analysis, based upon, as she described it, "arguments with my family, my teachers, and my friends."

In another example, in a semiurban school I observed a seventh grade Navajo boy who had a year earlier been referred to the school psychologist as hostile and uncooperative find remarkable inspiration in a project involving several media. The class was studying American history and the movement westward. Most students were reading and drawing maps. But this boy, along with a friend, tape-recorded their voices reading from some supplementary magazines and books, superimposed music (The Grand Canyon Suite) on their narration, ordered a film on the Louisiana Purchase from the catalogue in the principal's office, and made a grand combined presentation to their class. It was the hit of the semester—and it was also a remarkable turning point in the school career of that youngster.

Contributors to recent journals such as *Audiovisual Instruction* and *Educational Technology,* have begun to write about the new teacher and the changing role of the teachers in our public schools.* Contrary to the oft-heard caution that machines might take over the human role in the teaching-learning interactive process, there seems to be growing evidence that technical developments of educational

---

* See *Educational Technology,* February 1970, the entire issue, for its focus on "The Changing Role of the Teacher." Also see *Audiovisual Instruction,* February 1970, for its articles on inquiry learning, individualized study, self-paced learning, and the use of educational media.

ALL KINDS

OF COLORS

OF PEOPLE

Figure 3. *No War Toys for Young Writers and Illus-trators.* A page each from the two parts of a book that is half words inviting pictures, and half pictures inviting words.

No War Toys Book for Young Writers and Illustrators. No War Toys, Inc. Los Angeles, 1968. Reprinted by permission.

No War Toys Book for Young Writers and Illustrators. No War Toys, Inc. Los Angeles, 1968. Reprinted by permission.

media will enhance rather than impede the personalizing and the humanizing of our instruction.

Discovery   Since one person cannot force another person to integrate a concept into his behavioral makeup, discovery learning, which is knowledge or experience voluntarily appropriated by the learner, can become a focal point for all the other facets affecting curriculum that have been discussed in this chapter.

In a sense, all true learning is through discovery. Learners from preschool to graduate school are charmed by personal revelations. If they discover something, they have had to be involved in it, or to have been trying to seek it out. If they have had to seek it out, it must have been alluring enough to entice them. If it enticed them, it was speaking somehow to their private worlds: It was relevant. The concept of discovery as a key learning modality seems to pervade all of the several brief samples of curricular approaches we have just described.

Textbooks that speak to the perceptual world of the learner, either because they are created or chosen by him, have a chance to be relevant.

Language instruction can be organized so that every day in school affords an opportunity for verbal intercourse. Small-group, planned discussions, such as those suggested by William Glasser,* can offer opportunity for discovery of the nature of language and communication.

There are the same possibilities for learning human values and social skills in the classroom. Just as morality and civility cannot ultimately be legislated, neither can they be forced upon a learner. If the situations are such that human encounters occur, the bouncing of one's personality off one's peers in social interaction affords a wonderful chance to discover feelings and perceptions. All we need do is allow such interaction to go on in our schools.

One of the best strategies for discovery is to have children teach other children. It is perhaps the least coercive approach, and therefore the most open to free inquiry and discovery. The child-helper is perceived as less intimidating and so more freeing. The learner becomes more open to discoveries.

Creativity, of course, is virtually eliminated without the corollary strategy of discovery learning. One cannot be creative with another's structure, another's learning method, another's concepts or ideas.

---

* In his *Schools without Failure*. Harper and Row, New York, 1968.

Uniquely personal discoveries through cognitive and affective involvement lead to the creation of new concepts and new modes of behavior. The creative child—any child who is *being* creative—is constantly uncovering and discovering new combinations.

Discovery can be made through all the human senses—but only if opportunities are available. It therefore becomes necessary for teachers to be alert to all the media of stimulation. There must be no more days of the entire class facing front, the entire class reading silently and answering questions at the end of the chapter, the entire class doing the same thing at the same time. Children learn by discovering relationships in the environment around them; it is the *new* teacher's role to make that environment a multi-phasic, multi-sensoried one.

Children will *reach* for new ideas and new insights. I sometimes think that the major role of a good helper is to see to it that he does not get in their way.

A curriculum that is relevant cannot continue to perpetuate cultural exclusivity and superiority. A curriculum that is to be relevant must reexamine what has come to be its single-purpose emphasis, a preparation for financial independence. It must be flexible, many-faceted, and receptive to diverse individual goals. If a child and his family and his life style shout out to the schools that his is to be the life of the poet —our schools must be structured to accommodate this goal.

It would seem that our school curriculum-makers must ultimately decide whether or not they are to continue to determine the life styles of children. Or, as an alternative, maybe they will begin to take children where they are, culturally and aesthetically, and help them to develop whatever life style they know to the heights of their potentials.

Phrased another way, will our curriculum continue to be imposed externally, as if all children's needs and goals can be placed on a time-grid and an expectancy table, or will a truly intrinsic and psychological curricular model evolve? With powerless children, the latter is a necessity.

The Philadelphia Parkway Project, known as the "school without walls," is an example of an up-dated curricular approach. High school youngsters (120 in the pilot program) forged their own education by using the scientific, business, and cultural enterprises of their city, spending days, even weeks out in the city, guided (in groups of 15) by tutors, learning chemistry of gases at the gas company, statistics at an insurance company, and evolution at the Academy of Natural Sciences. A tribute to the flexible, very relevant curriculum is that 2000 youngsters applied for the 120 available positions.

Our questions asked earlier—whether children who had been over-powered by alienation and inadequacy have any chance to gain con-fidence and to gain power; whether such children can overcome the cultural bias they have known; and whether any curriculum no matter how relevant can stir them and speak to them—these questions are slowly but dramatically being answered by the youngsters themselves. Recent turmoil in the public schools, as early in the educational process as the junior high, announces to the society at large that lassitude and powerlessness are on the run. The children, backed by their parents, are demanding (and getting) meaningful courses of study and understanding, tuned-in teachers. We are in a curricular revolution. Let's hope our schools and their ministers will be the leaders and facilitators of it, not its obstructors and inhibitors.

Discussion to this point has alluded to the need for curriculum to offer children a chance to *think*. It has also implied that allowance must be made for the learning of feelings and values. In those contexts, it can be said that the curricular structure of our schools might very well include as its stated objectives more than just reading, writing, and arithmetic. Comic Steve Allen was the keynote speaker at a convention of counselors in Anaheim, California, in February 1969. He did not give a comical speech. He closed his remarks with the exhortation that our schools ought to teach: "readin', writin', 'rith-metic, thinkin', and lovin'."

Notes   1. Borton, Terry. "Reach, Touch and Teach," *Saturday Review,* January 18, 1969.

2. Bruner, Jerome S. "Learning and Thinking," in Don Hamachek, edi-tor, *Human Dynamics in Psychology and Education.* Boston: Allyn and Bacon, 1968, pp. 21–29.

3. Clark, Martha A. Final speech to participants NDEA Institute, Monte Corona, California, July 29, 1966. Reprinted by permission.

4. Cowles, Milly, editor. *Perspectives in the Education of Disadvantaged Children.* Cleveland: World, 1967.

5. Frost, J. L., and G. R. Hawkes, editors. *The Disadvantaged Child: Issues and Innovations.* Boston: Houghton Mifflin, 1966.

6. Gesell, Arnold L., and Frances L. Ilg. *The Child from Five to Ten.* New York and London: Harper, 1946.

7. Getzels, Jacob W., and Phillip W. Jackson. *Creativity and Intelligence: Explorations with Gifted Students.* London and New York: Wiley, 1962.

8. Gotkin, Lassar G. *Matrix Games.* New York: New Century, Educational Division, Meredith Corporation, 1967. Reprinted by permission.

9. Guilford, Joy Paul. *The Nature of Human Intelligence.* New York: McGraw-Hill, 1967.

10. Hubatch, Sister M. Antoninus, O.S.F. *Our Book,* San Xavier del Bac, Tucson, Arizona, 1968.

11. Hughes, Langston. "Dream Deferred." Copyright 1951 by Langston Hughes. Reprinted from *The Panther and the Leash,* by Langston Hughes, by permission of Alfred A. Knopf, Inc.

12. "Mose." (On the phonograph record, *J. W. Anderson Presents Kasandra.*)

13. *No War Toys Book for Young Writers and Illustrators.* No War Toys, Inc., Los Angeles, California, 1968.

14. Ortega y Gasset, Jose. *Mission of the University.* London: Routledge and Kegan Paul, 1946.

15. Rogers, Carl. "Personal Thoughts on Teaching and Learning," in Don Hamachek, editor, *Human Dynamics in Psychology and Education.* Boston: Allyn and Bacon, 1968.

16. Rosenthal, Robert and Lenore F. Jacobson. *Pygmalion in the Classroom; Teacher Expectation and Pupils' Intellectual Development.* New York: Holt, 1968.

17. Sprague, Jane, *Runaway Jerk.* Los Angeles City Schools Publication No. ESEA 4–8.

18. Thelen, Herbert Arnold, *et al. Classroom Grouping for Teachibility.* New York: Wiley, 1967.

19. Tuckman, Bruce W., and John L. O'Brian. *Preparing to Teach the Disadvantaged.* New York: Free Press, 1969.

20. *Voices of Youth.* Los Angeles City Schools, Publication No. ESEA 4–7.

21. Warner, Sylvia Ashton. *Teacher.* New York: Bantam Books, 1964.

Part Three

Teachers and the Poor

Chapter Seven

Indoctrination into Teaching

Just as the notion that education can
only be measured out in units
of semester hours has become a sacred
cow, so has the concept of the "course."
Higher education in America is course-
ridden . . . (and) seem(s) to be
almost totally committed to the
shibboleth of the "course" involving a
certain amount of time in a certain
room.

James B. Conant, in The Education of
American Teachers, *McGraw-Hill, New
York; 1963, pp. 78–79. Reprinted
by permission.*

In 1962, at the time that *The Other America,* (2) by Michael Harrington, was published, vast programs of compensatory education were initiated and an intense "war on poverty" in America began. In January 1969, Harrington returned to a consideration of what (if anything) had happened in America since his earlier investigations. In an article called "The Other America Revisited," (3) Harrington wrote that things were actually worse. While there had been a modest drop in the official poverty figures, the "over-the-line" poor seemed dangerously close to slipping back. The conditions of black Americans improved even more slowly than that of the poor in general. As of 1966, one-fourth of the children of America were living in poverty or hanging just above the official line. Harrington notes with resignation that "present evidence points to the melancholy conclusion that the 25 percent of the young who are poor, or near-poor, will have large families very much like the ones of which they are now members. If this is true, the current incidence of poverty among children will guarantee that, short of radical political decisions, the next generation in the other America will be even more numerous than this one." (3)

Mr. Harrington is telling America that the poor are going to be around for a while; that too little has been done to break their overpowering cycle of poverty; and that, believe it or not, it doesn't have to be that way. He notes in conclusion that "it is possible to make the massive planned social investments that would create the setting in which the poor would become more organized and determined to control their own political and economic destiny." (3) It seems that Mr. Harrington is saying the poor need to gain self-dignity and self-motivation, and there *is* something that powerful, affluent Americans can do to help—hinging upon the concept of "planned social investments." In the context of this book, such investments involve the schools, the teachers, and the formal educative process. But that educative process is worlds away from the poor.

Earlier, we considered schools as primary indoctrinating agents of the majority culture, and we examined ways in which the school environment might be structured to enhance the emergence of her powerless members. It now becomes our task to focus on the human personification—the personal agent—of the majority culture, and the ways in which that agent now functions compared to how he or she might function. The reference is, of course, to the teacher.

What effect have teachers had in perpetuating the denigration of the so-called undercultures in America? How have teachers been trained to become indoctrinating agents? What is our standard teacher-education exposure like? Can an impact be made upon the cycle of poverty through restructuring this one "planned social investment"?

Given today's school structure and today's teacher attitudes and approaches, a valuable education for the powerless is impossible. This is an indictment of the entire system, not merely its programs for the poor. The fact is that most of our students from kindergarten—even preschools—through college are virtually powerless with respect to their formal education. Much of this is due to the way our teachers have been trained. (Some exciting changes have occurred in teacher education programs, however, and some prototypes will be explored later in this writing.)

The very notion (which we reverently cling to) of "teacher training" as the official rubric of the preparation process illustrates our misdirection. For me, "training" is what one does to animals and more recently to machines. Then they can continue to do that for which they were trained over and over and over and over and over. . . .

The diversity of human beings, the need for creative thought, the dynamic and fluid interaction, the delightful variability of behavior—all require an innovative and sensitive human facilitator as a teacher. These same variables utterly destroy the "trainer's" capacity to be effective.

The effect of producing teachers who have been trained but not sensitized (and are not sensi*tive*) is that our classrooms have been conducted in much the same way as a circus is conducted by a ring-master. Each animal and each piece of equipment is in its proper place; each animal knows what signals require which response; each performer is rewarded for his conformity; and each performer is dismally unexpressive and powerless. One cannot help but contrast the center ring of the circus with the promenade section of the San Diego Zoo, where dozens of monkeys startle the world with their varied and melodious expressive shrieks and calls; or an even more obvious comparison—with the freedom, spontaneity, and unquestioned power of the animals cavorting in their natural jungle setting.

Some may reply, of course, that we are not dealing with animals. Children are active creatures with little social self-control. There must be discipline or *no* learning will occur. School is a place for the orderly pursuit of knowledge. Teachers are adults with special skills in controlling and guiding the young. . . . Each of these sentences is progressively more coercive in its implications and less child-centered in its perceptual view.

The world of the child is actually amazingly well ordered. Children have a great deal of self-control and are, in fact, tenacious in their attention and devotion when they are stimulated. Very little learning occurs under strict control or heavy discipline ("We must have more tolerance for noise and confusion"). Though most teachers today

The Notion of Teacher Training

have special *training* in controlling and guiding the young, they have little special skill in it. There is a difference, and our schools' failure to be relevant points to it.

So, the cumulative effect of our entire "training" program of teachers has been that generations of Americans are being nudged to physical maturity with, in the terminology of the Lewin, Lippitt, and White study, (5) *autocratic followership personalities.* Another way of saying it is that our children are growing up with urges to conformity (although, one hopes, some are rebellious), with feelings of alienation (although, one hopes, some have found an intimacy with each other), with feelings of powerlessness (although, one hopes, a few are condemning the process of indoctrination). (Today, some of our youngsters are teaching our teachers; with the braver ones, the less subordinate, the less supplicating, providing some sparks of hope that the system is not all bad and that if they were able to survive it perhaps it could still be salvaged. Perhaps with *their* guidance there will be some changes. Yet, the majority today remain its victims.)

The earlier statement—that teachers have special training in controlling and guiding the young, but little special skill—needs some expanding. Teacher training institutions have units on discipline. In fact, some have special courses in classroom management and control. Most teachers-in-training are taught techniques which they can use for specific problem situations that come up. Example after example of such specific situations often are employed so that teachers will have many simulated experiences prior to the real thing. But the rather predictable result of such drill and training is that our teachers become distrustful of their own feelings about children. They have been patterned so rigidly by the artificiality of their training that they have learned to rely on outside models for their classroom "control, discipline, and management." They have literally become desensitized to their own human reaction to unique situations and their own spontaneity of action.

The products of such programs do poorly in controlling and guiding the students because they are not basically honest in what they do. They do what they do as part of the game one learns to play during the process of becoming a teacher. Teacher training has taught our teachers how to ignore their own instincts in relating to children.

Our training institutions have done a good job of convincing their trainees that school is a "versus situation." That is, that when a teacher enters the class, it is *her, versus the kids. . . .* And after all, the teacher is told, who knows better, you (well-trained, older, more experienced) or the kids? And so—because you are right, you are wiser, you *have been trained*—you clamp the lid on, and the pernicious practice of autocratic followership is begun. How much more enhancing it would be if different initial questions were asked; if, instead of, "who knows better, you by yourself, or me by myself?" we asked "who knows better, you by yourself, me by myself, or all of us together?"

Of course, some would argue that the most important aspect of teacher training is subject-matter mastery. All other aspects of class-room business are peripheral to that. I would like to attack such a notion as fundamentally naive and creating a false dichotomy as well. The more profound and more positive position is that knowledge of subject matter is indispensable to the well-prepared teacher. But so is his awareness of himself, his understanding of principles of develop-ment, learning, motivation, and emotional variability, and his feelings about children and their education. A "prepared" teacher is prepared in all these ways—for no subject matter can be transmitted in a class-room climate of repression or hostility or insecurity. Arthur Combs recently wrote: "What is often not understood by many critics of modern education is that teachers rarely fail because of lack of knowledge of subject matter. When they fail it is almost always be-cause they have been unable to transmit what they know so that it makes a difference to students." (1)

The phrase *teacher training* ought to be considered a misnomer; rather, we ought to begin to speak, as does Combs, of the professional education of teachers. (1) Teacher training has created generations of classroom managers, schooled in gimmickry and frightened to death of their children and of their own feelings. Teacher training has created defensive teachers, teachers who in their anticipation of dis-ruption oppress and coerce their students. And teacher training has failed to produce democratic climates for learning, and subsequently failed to produce learners who are democratic.

And here we sit! One-fourth of our school children are in families that live in or close to a culture of poverty. Many of them, and many others, live in families with varied (sometimes rural) life styles. Teachers come from the dominant and culturally exclusive middle group in America. They are trained to become the rulers of their domains. They are oppressive to most children; they are intolerant of difference among children within even their own ethnic and cultural phylum; they are misled about the nature of learning and insist on a uniform structuring of subject matter for all their learners; and they confront their classroom situations expecting hostility. Imagine the helplessness that overpowers the children of the *poor* when they encounter the typically trained American public school teacher!

What our teachers do in schools reflects what was done to them during their preparation. And most of what has been done to them violates everything that is known about communication and learning

Training through Course Work

theory. Most of what they have experienced on their way to becoming teachers has occurred within several four-walled rooms, using several books as reference authorities, hearing several lecturers who are experienced authorities, and occasionally interacting with their fellow students in order to "share" ideas. In short, so it seems, our teachers pretty much learn how to teach through their formal course work. . . .

Actually, the formal course work should provide no more than a catalyst which would help to stimulate the more authentic aspects of teacher preparation. (The reference here is to all sorts of course work, and not solely to that course work officially listed in the catalogues as education courses.) No doubt, our teachers would progress without such heavy focus on formal course work—indeed, perhaps without it would be more sensitive and better able to work with children. Yet we continue to insist that the formal course work is really what does the job in preparing better teachers. *How* does course work act to desensitize large numbers of dedicated and eager teachers-to-be? Let us try a brief list and then expand upon it. . . .*

1. Students are assembled, for the most part, in neat rows, facing the professor. (The more adept learn, by the time they are juniors, to sleep quite well sitting up with their eyes wide open.)
2. Professors carefully avoid personal contact with their students (teachers-to-be), because their objectivity and the equity of their evaluations would otherwise suffer.
3. Many professors are quite steeped in their own subject area, but their skill at providing any incentives for their students consists primarily of *telling* them all about what they know.
4. There is a weary and dreary notion among professors that what is important to them is also going to be important to their students; and so teaching becomes a process of insisting that students master what their professors have mastered—some make it quite clear that *they* are personal role models for their students.
5. Course work for teachers-to-be is structured as if the whole of human and social evolution occurred in stratified and isolated capsules; students learn, for example, the history of the eighteenth century in one course, the art of the eighteenth century in another course, the music of the eighteenth century in another course, and its psychology in another course (small wonder that our students leave college totally

---

* We must keep in mind that as these criticisms are written, they are being responded to. There is evidence that significant change is coming about in many institutions around the country. The model of a teacher "product" herein described will be, I hope, well on the road toward extinction by the time these words are read.

compartmentalized in their understanding of world events); they sometimes know when the American Revolution took place, but are completely frustrated about the impact of that event upon, for example, the composers or the journalists of that day, and vice versa.

6. Course work is, in most instances, temporally stifling and rigid; if, by chance, an incisive, stimulating, relevant interchange does occur, it is most often cut off at the 50-minute mark—professors rarely find time to go out on the lawn with the class to continue their argument, nor can students remain, surrounded as they are by their own inflexible schedules.

7. In college as in public schools, few examples can today be cited of courses (in all subject areas) that speak to the contributions, heritage, and present condition of American minority groups.

8. And finally, formal course work, structured as it inevitably is, convinces students that what they must all exalt and strive toward is the successful completion of other-directed, specified activities and their culminating evaluations, the grades; our teachers-to-be are so well versed in subordinating their curiosity to the assignments of their professors that they cannot help but themselves become teachers who hammer their students into conformity.

Of course, such a list could be made larger. But this short list illuminates a certain pervasive emphasis that most certainly will produce teachers who are as insensitive to their young students as their teachers were to them.

Our teachers-to-be are typically placed in a relationship with their professors which accentuates the distance between them. They are taught *at*—lectured to—for the most part, and the distance makes teacher versus learner a reality in the college classroom. *That* becomes the model for our new teachers.

A singularly distressing aspect of our teachers-to-be is that so very many of them are actually unaware of the indoctrinating nature of their experiences. They have been so nurtured in styles of authoritarian followership, so conditioned to accept routine and control and dictation that their personalities have become zippered tight. They come to accept, indeed enshrine, the "good" teacher as one who is in complete control. Just as the cycle of poverty cannot be easily broken, neither can the cycle of authoritarianism. And generations of children grow up to teach new generations all about democracy through the most undemocratic means. Small wonder they fail.

Our teachers-to-be have learned that their college teachers refused to create with them an intimacy of spirit, a communion of intellectual and emotional adventure. Thus have they learned to avoid closeness with their young students. They are sometimes exposed (in Psychological Foundations of Education courses) to discovery approaches to the mysteries of the world, but those by no means comprise the overwhelming balance of their experience.

Because of the remarkable jealousy and sense of self-preservation of each dynastic segment of academia, prospective teachers do not have a cohesive or a developmental understanding of the world in which they live. The lessons of the past do not influence their actions, because those lessons are a jigsaw puzzle of jurisdictional shrapnel, never once pulled together into a meaningful "weltanschauung." The findings of social science (indeed, some remarkable research discoveries!) have little influence on the operation of our teachers-to-be, because they see them having no influence on the way their professors have been working with them.*

Our teachers-to-be cannot be culturally expansive in their outlook; they have so few primary examples of teachers who have appreciated the potential diversity of American life. They have had so few teachers of their own who have not themselves been indoctrinated into a kind of antidemocratic oversimplification of the tenets of the good life. And, sadly, our teachers-to-be are woeful victims of all the overpowering stimuli in their training which cajole them into sacrificing what they are really interested in for what is *supposed* to be learned. They are wooed away from the delirium of discovery toward the doldrums of duty. And that process leaves them utterly and dismally conditioned into demanding the same kinds of behavior from their students.

When John Holt describes with insight how children fail, (4) he is by implication also telling us how teachers fail. He is telling us how, as the principal vehicle for training teachers, formal course work has been an utter disaster; how its emphases have diverted the real notion of how one prepares to relate significantly to young learners. Teachers who are so trained emerge with totally distorted beliefs and expectations about their own students:

Teachers and schools tend to mistake good behavior for good character. What they prize above all else is docility, suggestibility; the child who will do what he is told; or even better, the child who will do what is wanted without even having to be told. They value most in children what children least value in themselves. (4)

Powerless children do not resist such damaging expectations from their teachers; they all too often give in to the mystery and the con-

---

* The University of Pittsburgh Teacher Training Model, for one, is a striking exception to this condition. Their program of individualizing the teacher-instruction pattern, and providing an environment which they hope will be the kind the teacher would create with his students, is an example of enlightenment in teacher education.

fusion of teachers' odd requirements. And so each generation inherits the emotional, intellectual, and spiritual debility of the one before it.

Teacher training has ignored the sensitization of students to their own feelings and to the impact their personalities have on others. The course work our teachers-to-be experience prepares them to be intolerant of cultural diversity, inflexible in their structure, overpowering in their discipline ("the strong teacher is a teacher who tolerates no nonsense"), ignorant of unusual belief systems and alien life values, and totally inured to the subverbal or feeling-level communication their students so desperately invoke.

When ample course work has been absorbed by aspiring young teachers, it is time to expose them to their practicum. Usually, this involves two semesters of mornings spent in a classroom at the secondary level, and one semester of full days or segments of days spent in the classroom at the elementary level. The university provides a supervising professor and the public school provides a master teacher.

**Training through
Student Teaching**

One young woman recently described her supervised, guided student-teaching experience this way:

I cried myself to sleep every night. They weren't at all interested in my relationship with the children. They kept telling me to use pins instead of thumbtacks and kept showing me how the bulletin boards were supposed to be organized. Every evening I had reading charts to print up and my printing had to be letter perfect, just so high and just so thick. They were so worried I wouldn't learn their routine because they said the children get restless when the familiar routine is broken. This was the most uncreative five months I've ever spent in anything!

Another teacher-to-be was student teaching in a junior high school class in journalism. She described what happened to her:

Well this teacher never even studied journalism, he was an English major. And he just didn't think much of the kids. He kept saying they were dumb and that he had to keep a tight hold on them. About half of the kids in his room were black and yet one day he brought in a study about Negro intelligence and said that it confirmed all of his beliefs and that there was no doubt in his mind about the genetic differential. And about that time there were some marches and uprisings around the city in the junior and senior high schools and our youngsters were quite restless. All he could say to me was something about what "your liberal philosophy does for you—all those kids being permitted to disrupt our institutions." The thing was, when I suggested that I would have the students write editorials

about aspects of the school unrest that they felt were important, he stifled
the assignment by having them finish his incomplete titles: "Public School
Disruption Is Harmful because. . . ." or "Outside Agitators on the
Campuses Cause. . . ."

I recently listened to a briefing of a college class of teachers-to-be
about to spend a semester at a junior high school. The principal and
vice principals described the school, its policies, its routines, and its
disciplinary procedures. They told about how proud they were of their
racial balance (about one-third caucasian, one-third black, one-third
Mexican-American). Then they described how, when school was
over, the blacks all went home "over there," the whites "over there,"
and the Chicanos "over there," all in different directions. The principal told about the special, federally funded programs they had and all
the extra equipment they were allowed because of their minority
population. One of the vice principals took time to describe how the
venetian blinds should be kept, and cautioned his listeners to avoid
standing in front of the light because it gave the children headaches
if they had to gaze at the teacher's silhouette during the lesson. The
hour-and-a-half briefing was once suspended while the principal went
to his office to address all the students in the school over the loudspeaker. He spoke for 14 minutes to 1700 students, all of whom were
sitting in classrooms around the school, all of whom were doing
exactly the same thing at that time: listening to a voice from a box.
The principal told them about the PTA drive, about which home
rooms were tops in recruiting, about which home rooms were winning
the contest. And he told them about the vandalism at the bungalow
over the weekend, "which would not be tolerated." Then he told
them how proud he was of "our school" and his high hopes for its
reputation as the finest junior high in the city. . . . The entire briefing had an unexpectedly premature ending when the three administrators were called away to investigate some problem in the quad
during nutrition. The process of "fitting in" new members to the
system had begun.

These examples do not represent isolated and unusual glimpses
through the windows of our schools. When college students enter
student teaching they *do* encounter such routines, such attitudes, and
such insensitivity. One secondary school principal refused to permit
students to student teach in the art department of his school because
". . . there are no teachers in our art department I would care to
have any young teacher be exposed to. Boys are uncontrolled in some
of those classes, and the leadership is quite poor." Yet, the students
at that school (largely Mexican-American) were most appreciative
of the specific teacher whose boys were "uncontrolled." He wore a

beard and an open shirt. He was Anglo, but he spoke Spanish. He was educated, but he lived in the barrio where the children lived. He was sensitive, unstructured, nonconforming, and thoroughly loved. And no student teachers were allowed in his class.

Student teaching is the formalized, on-the-job aspect of teacher indoctrination. When student teachers conclude their time at a given school, they are rated by their master teacher and their supervisor. They are rated on such criteria as classroom management, discipline, knowledge of subject matter, ability to use methods, and a kind of superficial rapport with students. It is interesting that no one attempts to assess the deeper quality of their relationships with students, their empathy for student needs, their sensitivity toward relationships between students, their seeming alertness to principles of motivation and human learning, their spontaneity, their creativity and flexibility, their love of people, their joy or verve for life, their restlessness, their inquisitiveness and challenging nature, their resistance to dogma and to routine. . . .

When student teachers conclude their time at any given school, they are also ready to begin the process of interviewing for a job. Often the school where they did their student teaching will get first crack at them and will choose them or not, depending upon their compatibility with the existing system. Repeatedly, a potentially imaginative and very human teacher is not selected by his training school because he is "a bit too unusual," or "he wouldn't fit in." In this way each school perpetuates its own style by stifling the potential for dissent and insuring the prevention of change. From another perspective, it can be said that each school thus continues to be static instead of dynamic, irrelevant instead of exciting.*

Lately, an even more unfortunate development has occurred, one which leaves the most needy schools floundering for lack of creative new talent. Young, expressive, potentially gifted teachers are beginning to interview the principals, instead of the other way around; thoughtful, restless young people are beginning to discriminate against school districts that restrict and oppress. In one sense, that could force the schools to change—at least, enough to attract capable teachers. But largely because so many of the teacher trainees wish to

---

* It is interesting that political leaders more and more are castigating teachers, administrators, and schools for disproportionately hiring so-called "liberal" teachers, especially at the college level. They claim that this amounts to indoctrination into a liberal philosophy. If any message is at all apparent from this present writing, it is that the exact opposite is true. Regardless of political bent, most teachers, when it comes to education and their relationship with students, are unbelievably reserved and conservative, "up-tight" and conforming, static and nonexperimental, obedient and institutionally patriotic.

work in or near large population centers, and because teacher supply is catching up with demand, such districts have been able to find enough people to staff their schools. The distinct calamity is that most of those districts in large cities tend to assign most of the compliant young teachers to the ghetto areas. Thus, excellence and innovation continue to elude the schools of the center city.

Children of the poor see so few people in the schools who can speak their language or who can understand them. In the past, by the time a Negro or a Mexican-American had gone through the credentialing process of becoming a teacher, he had been indoctrinated so completely into the established mold that he was no longer a "black" or a "Chicano." Part of the training process was to make him over into an acceptable middle-class teacher, who reflected the typical ideals of the dominant culture. Student teaching for any member of the poor has always meant a rejection of the culture from which he comes, an absorption of "the way things are done," a disdain for those who don't seem to try to make it ("After all, you came from that background and look at you"), and an adoption of the ethic that hard work will pay off. But there are signs that the poor who come from minority ethnic groups are no longer willing to trade off their identity for a badge in what they now consider a society of questionable value. Through this intrepid revolution by the formerly powerless, the majority culture is being forced to take a hard look at all its educative procedures. The training process called student teaching is one of the first to need reexamination.

Lesson Plans

Closely related to the process of student teaching is the procedure of making lesson plans. Not only must student teachers make out daily lesson plans, but in many schools so must new teachers. (I recall that in my first public school teaching assignment, with a class of seventh-grade youngsters who were supposed to be mentally retarded, I was required to submit a weekly lesson plan to a designated senior teacher. In practice, I discovered that the children pulled the class in so many different directions that the advance plans were all but useless. I later found it expedient to make up a hypothetical plan for the entire semester, week by week, on a large cardboard poster, and by way of placating the supervisor, copying down the segment for each week as it approached and turning it in to her. In all honesty, the daily activity seldom had much to do with the semester plot.)

There should be a distinction between a teacher's establishing certain goals for and with his students, and formulating daily lesson plans. There is no quarrel with the notion that the teacher will structure the environment in some given way—whether through arbitrary imposition of subject-matter drill or through his own, more personal influence. This structuring will no doubt be a product of his philosophy about children, about school, and about learning. But if his philosophy holds that children perceive the world in unique ways and that relevancy is highly personal and emergent, the external application of subject matter through lesson plans will utterly fail to relate to the students' actual needs. Yet, as it is today, lesson plans are required, and by this alone teachers-to-be are misguided about the way children are motivated to learn.

From my own vantage point, virtually every student teacher who has gone on into teaching has reacted negatively toward lesson plans. The notion of an extrinsic outline, rigidly adhered to and unilaterally composed, becomes stultifying to the creativity of the teacher. For the same reasons, lesson plans inhibit the students from daring to bring up what is on the tips of their tongues. No doubt, teachers who read this have had the experience of entering a classroom at least once in their careers and asking their students "what's on your mind?" The torrent of emotion and thought that erupts is often astounding, and teachers are left amazed at what the youngsters had been holding in.

I have heard a college professor tell about how he had been leading the students in his education class through critically important areas of discussion for several weeks. On alternate days, they were visiting and observing in the public schools. While he felt that what he was discussing with them was always important, he had never thought to include open time for the students each time the class met. Finally, one bold young man told him that he was sorry if it interrupted the professor's plans, and all that, but he wanted to tell the class something very important about his school observation and see what they thought about it. The professor, later that day, exuberantly told his colleagues about the ". . . best class session we've had all semester! I was able to join and suggest resources and ideas so that more learning theory was discussed today than in all the other meetings combined!" Following a lesson plan would have totally failed to "catch the teachable moment," "deal with emerging, dynamic, relevant problems," and "recognize that learning is highly personal and intrinsic."

Lesson plans as general guides for the teacher and his students, composed by the teacher *with* his students, have some organizational merit; lesson plans as plots for daily activities merely add to the misguided process of indoctrination into teaching.

The concept of grading, if we really face it, is attached to the exaltation of competition as the American way; perhaps that should be amended to read, *free and open* competition. It hardly behooves

The Process of Grading

the purpose of this writing to launch an indiscriminate attack on the American notion of competition, but a tacit belief that such competition is most often free and open definitely needs some investigation. Another aspect of grading which should be explored is the attendant axiom that by the processes of evaluation and comparison, some performers are bound to fail. What about that failure? Is it either necessary or healthy?

Teachers-to-be have been compared to others since (and even before) their formal schooling began. By the time they become teachers, the indoctrination into competitiveness is complete. They know only one way: to see how well each student can do in comparison with others. It is incidental that the children of the poor rarely do as well as the others. "They must learn it in school," our teachers are told. "Society is highly competitive and so our youngsters must learn to compete if they are going to make it." *

Oddly enough, there are signs that young people today are resisting that notion, and are seeking and finding intimacy and closeness with each other. Young people of today talk about love-ins and about going back to the noncompetitive Indian way. They talk about "being there for somebody"; about encounter or sensitivity experiences. They talk about and examine the deeper nature of man—aside from the form his so-called civilization has given him. And yet, their resistance is isolated and specific, and the majority of our population appears to continue in the quest for dominance.

Dominance over what? It is highly probable that, appealed to on a deeper level of feeling, most Americans would not exalt the ranking process of human beings, the process which sets up certain arbitrary criteria of "superior" and others equally arbitrary of "inferior." As standards of living for most Americans go up and the "good life" is experienced, it is likely that there is less and less need for the affluent (of spirit as well as possessions) to perpetuate an artificial hierarchy. Yet, instead of being sensitive to that deeper growth and maturity in our population, to that "coming-of-age-in-America," our schools continue to operate as if we live in a frontier era. They continue to operate in a framework of laissez-faire competition, while the society, at least in its deeper processes, moves toward an organized "co-operacy." We are saying that the schools by their function of grading

---

* Jack R. Gibb, former Resident Fellow at the Western Behavioral Science Institute in California, in a speech to secondary school administrators in 1969, challenged such a notion. He said that such a point of view, with its attendant concepts of leadership and aggressiveness, ". . . prepares the child for life, but for a life that's leaving us, for a world that was, for a society of the past." He went on to call for more "team building" and "cooperative problem-solving" in our schools.

contend that they reflect society's—that is, industry's—desires. "Corporations want to know who the *best* students are." We are also saying that, being on the forefront of knowledge, our schools should be sensitive to the subtleties of progress, and should indeed *lead* society into new dimensions of humanness.

As it is today, competition is not free and open. Since all Americans are not equally blessed, the competition we reverently cling to as the American way is shamefully undemocratic in its application to Americans who are culturally different. In most instances, the poor find themselves without the tools needed to compete equally (and no one allows for that), and find themselves failing. That revered competition is a major contributor to the perpetuation of powerlessness among many Americans. It is only when Americans who are powerful have been willing to give up some of their power (cooperation!), to be deliberately noncompetitive, that powerless Americans have begun to feel adequate and to move into emotional and personal health.

Grading implies success, and it implies failure. When one is constantly compared with someone else, it is either favorably or unfavorably, as a success or as a failure. Do we set up arbitrary ways for children to fail who otherwise might grow up with many feelings of adequacy and accomplishment? Are we not told that the world is hard and cruel and judgmental? (Of course our schools help to keep it that way!) If so, then our children will certainly encounter much failure after leaving school. Why can they not build margins of good feelings in school so that failure in the hard and callous world will not destroy them? Why can they not have so many experiences that reinforce their concepts of their own abilities and their own goodness that they *will* believe in themselves—the potential criticism of others be hanged!

And yet, a note of optimism. . . . Some colleges and universities have experimented boldly with the whole concept of the letter grade as an indication of achievement. At one institution, an experiment was initiated where, at the discretion of the student, he could enroll in any or all of his classes on a "pass—no credit" basis. Note that it is not pass-fail, which leaves a negative evaluation on the student's record. In pass—no credit, a student either achieves the desired goal (the teacher's or his own, depending on the operating philosophy in the classroom) or he does not. If he does not, then he may want to re-try his study in a certain area, or he may decide to avoid it. In any case, the negative imputation of the "fail" grade is removed.

A final point about grading has an ironic twist to it. It is the thought of Arthur Combs, and is quoted here because it seems to me that it shows unusual candidness and insight:

It is indeed a shame if, with all the richness of the American language, we are reduced to evaluating a student's promise in terms of A, B, C, D, or F! The college placement office is keenly aware that this is by no means enough and so requires much fuller descriptions of students to supply to prospective employers. As a consequence, the placement office, whose contact with the student may be for no more than ten minutes, knows him better than the college which has lived with him for four or five years! (1)

Whether competition and evaluation will become anachronistic as our society grows in its sensitivity and its humanity, is a moot point. But certainly, as Combs makes so clear, even within the existing structure, our approach to the evaluation of one human being by another can be so much more personalized and so much less mechanistic, so much deeper as a vehicle in ultimately enhancing the person being evaluated, and so much less an obvious criticism.

The Notion of Homework

Our teachers have been indoctrinated with the belief that assignments of work at home after school will somehow add to the diligence, devotion, training, and knowledge of students. Sadly, it has worked so that very close to the opposite has occurred.

Homework has been an influential factor in negatively reinforcing school activities. Children who are frustrated at the blandness and dullness of their school routines find such an influence following them even into their homes and bedrooms. They resent their schools and they resent their homework and both become less pertinent to their real feelings and their deeper motivations.

A youngster from a family that lives in a culturally different style, perhaps a culturally rural life pattern, finds the typical approach to homework stultifying and prejudicial. Very likely he will not have an "isolated and quiet place to study," a "well-lighted, clean, flat-surfaced, distraction-free cubicle." Nor is the homework content such that he can (or would want to) share it with or get help from his family.

Work of an intellectually challenging nature could very well be an enhancing takehome experience for children of the poor. And, carefully and wisely created, such assignments might indeed offer an opportunity to involve an entire family in educational activity—the whole family zestfully digging in, being nourished. Obviously, such activities would necessitate much prethought, much learning on the teacher's part about his students and their life styles, much careful examination, and, let's hope, some insight into the family living of his youngsters.

Now homework is the leftovers, drill time. Homework is the punishment—more if you are a slow worker in class, less if you are fast. Most teachers are trained to accept and follow, and few have ever thought about the entire concept of homework and what it is that homework might accomplish.

In this writing there has most certainly been a negative tone about education as it is. But I hope if the reader is as sensitive as one might imagine, he will see, even to this point, all kinds of wild shafts of light which knife through the darkness and give promise of a better day. And if through the system as it currently exists, with all its oppressive qualities, some young people have managed to emerge creative and challenging and pestiferous, there must be a certain amount of flexibility—at least enough for the aggressive to take advantage of.

A Final Notion

And certainly, to those teachers who have indeed struggled all these years to be facilitators for their youngsters, who have lived and loved their pupils' lives and loves, who have felt the tragedy it has been to be different in America's schools—to those teachers perhaps this writing is a compliment. Perhaps they will find an "aha" or a "eureka" as they read these words.

We have already alluded to change. The University of Pittsburgh program of individualizing instruction for teachers-in-training is but one example of several institutional changes and innovations that are progressing. In the Introduction to the Model, Chapter One of the Research Report on the Pittsburgh program, the following statement serves as a hope and a model: "[This] model proposes that the teacher will be instructed by a professional faculty using the same principles and practices of individualized instruction that the teacher will subsequently use with pupils." (6) The report defines individualized instruction as learning experiences which ". . . are tailor-made to suit [each student's] learning requirements and his characteristics as a learner." (6)

Other universities and colleges (nine in all) have engaged in similar research, which has been federally funded, in attempts to swing their programs of teacher preparation into line with the needs and realities of today's education. These programs must indeed be viewed optimistically.

A final notion about indoctrination must be mentioned. Most people who read these words would consider themselves good Americans. Most teachers would consider themselves good teachers. By that they mean that they believe in and profess to live the democracy that America is supposed to stand for. Most would be reluctant to apply any of the narrowness portrayed in the previous descriptions to them or their way of living. But just as I must catch myself over and over from thinking and writing about culturally diverse youngsters as *the disadvantaged* (our chauvinism is so powerful!), so do others carry with them the remnants of cultural exclusivity. Just as I must resist wanting to "rush in and fix things" for learners instead of believing that true learning occurs through discovery, so do others play the part of the manipulator or the manager.

Teachers-to-be are indoctrinated into a narrow way of perceiving children and the educative experience. But the indoctrination is so very much an intrinsic part of our entire middle-class aura, that it most often eludes the conscious awareness of our teachers. And so who, after all, can admit that he is racist, prejudicial, harmful in his attitudes, or indeed even narrow in his outlook, when all he does is what everyone (his former teachers, his colleagues, the public) expects of him?

But I believe that I would fail utterly if I stopped at criticism, if I stopped at highlighting the failures of our present system. If meaningful education is to exist for powerless Americans, for Americans beginning to feel their identity, then positive approaches must be explored. Teachers must learn that theirs is the task of releasing the creative potential of the formerly withdrawn, the humiliated, the unmotivated, the criticized, the beautifully different and desperate and powerless children in our schools.

Perhaps the chapter which follows can make a meager beginning in exploring ways to achieve such goals.

Notes

1. Combs, Arthur W. *The Professional Education of Teachers.* Boston: Allyn and Bacon, 1965, p. 20. Reprinted by permission.

2. Harrington, Michael. *The Other America.* New York: MacMillan, 1962.

3. Harrington, Michael. "The Other America Revisited," p. 36–41. Reprinted by permission, from the January 1969 issue of *The Center Magazine,* a publication of the Center for the Study of Democratic Institutions in Santa Barbara, California.

4. Holt, John. *How Children Fail.* New York, p. 136. Copyright © 1964 by Pitman Publishing Corporation. Reprinted by permission of Pitman Publishing Corporation.

5. Lewin, Kurt, R. Lippitt, and R. K. White. "Patterns of Aggressive

Behavior in Experimentally Created 'Social Climates,' " *Journal of Social Psychology,* 10, 1939, pp. 271–299.

6. Research Report No. 0–8–089020–3309(010) *A Model of Teacher Training for the Individualization of Instruction.* Washington, D.C.: U.S. Department of Health, Education, and Welfare, Office of Education, Bureau of Research, October 1968, p. 2.

Chapter Eight

Teachers as Facilitators

Noise, noise, noise, yes. But if you don't
like noise, don't be a teacher. Because
children are noisy animals. . . . But
it's a natural noise and therefore
bearable. True, there is an occasional
howl of rage, a shout of accusation,
soprano crying and the sound of
something falling, but there is also a
voice raised in joy, someone singing
and the break, break, break of laughter.
In any case it's all expulsion of energy
and as such, a help. I let anything
come . . . within safety; but I *use*
it. . . .

It's just that I like the lid off. I like
seeing what's there. I like unpredicta-
bility and gaiety and interesting
people, however small, and funny

things happening and sweet, and everything that life is, uncovered. I hate
covers of any kind. I like the true
form of living, even in school.

Sylvia Ashton Warner. Teacher, *Simon
and Schuster, Inc., New York, 1963,
pp. 104 and 106. Reprinted by
permission of Simon and Schuster, Inc.,
and Martin Secker and Warburg
Limited.*

People who become teachers place themselves, like other professionals (and nonprofessionals), in a helping relationship to others. Almost always, the helper appears to have a distinguishing characteristic which influences and guides his activities—the quality of *caring* for the other or others he encounters.

Carl Rogers, the humanist psychologist, uses the word "prizing" in describing a significant trait in a relationship between a helper and his companion: (15) The helper believes that his beneficiary is a person of worth, that he is valuable as a human being. It has been postulated that if growth and some kind of improvement in the quality of living is to occur within the seeker of help, the helper must somehow *come across* to him as really caring, as prizing him as a unique and worthwhile person. The trait of caring must be *perceived* by the learner or seeker. . . .

When one purports to be in a helping relationship to others, but does not come across as caring about those others, he does not merely fail to help, he actually does some damage to those he is trying to help. It is not unlikely that this has been the case in the teaching-learning relationships in our public schools, especially when the learner is a member of a culturally different group.

But the very awareness, among some people, of the potential for a helping or a therapeutic relationship growing out of honest caring permits optimism. If teachers are to help powerless children grow into self-directing, confident people, it seems implicit that such teachers must be able to *prize* their students, that teacher preparation must seek to identify and to encourage such teachers; and that institutions which engage in teacher education must be kept from diverting or distorting those primary qualities from maturing.

A good teacher (for all children) is a human being who is himself secure enough to allow freedom to explore, open enough to appreciate the radiant beauty of all human cultures, serene enough to tolerate confusion, and sensitive enough to feel and sense the deeper messages that children are constantly sending. In this chapter, our aim is to explore ways in which teachers-to-be can retain or achieve qualities such as sensitivity, honesty, empathy, flexibility. . . .

Becoming a Facilitator: A Total Experience

So far, we have presented two basic themes: the spectrum of powerlessness and the dominant culture's interaction with it; the foibles and the potentials of public education. In this section a knitting together of the two themes, I hope, can begin. Presuming that educators have become sensitized to the culture of poverty and the diverse cultures among our children, and presuming they are aware that new curricular approaches and new community activity are

critical factors in advancements toward power and pride—presuming
all this, what sort of groundwork or structuring can best prepare
new teachers for optimum functioning in implementing such awareness?

Becoming a facilitator cannot be a piecemeal, course-by-course,
disjointed operation. It cannot be an operation divorced from the
community and the impact of today's urban living. The total experience of becoming a helper to today's children must be cast in a
setting that is intimate and continually reinforcing. A facilitator can
become sensitive (to others *and* himself) by being exposed to
situations where he must act and interact in sensitive ways. Consider
the following as an example of one possible program.

The Live-in
Institute

With the National Defense Education Act of 1958 came funding
for some experiments in education. Hundreds of teacher institutes
were conducted all over the country—so many, and with such
predictable formats, that they soon became fair game for the same
kinds of satire and stereotyping that the more standard forms of
in-service education had always received. Yet, some of the new
institutes tracked new country and did, indeed, ring new bells. Why
were some effective and others the same old medicine?

The institutes which seemed to speak to teachers in meaningful
ways contained aspects of intimacy and close interaction which were
qualitatively different from the others. Members became deeply
involved with other members and with their leaders and counselors.
They were few large group sessions and many smaller encounter
situations, both in college classrooms and in real-life surroundings.
Members became involved in activity with children, with families,
with each other; they lived in dormitories or in clustered housing
where discourse went on all the time, sometimes throughout the
night. Professors and community-resource people sat in informal
and often intimate settings with groups of members; participants
formed bonds of closeness with their groups and with individuals.
The community and, in effect, the real world were exposed to the
institute members, many of whom were teachers of urban, culturally
diverse children.

Though some few were for an academic year, generally these
institutes were summertime affairs with little provision for year-long
continuance. In informal kinds of follow-up, I have observed that
teachers exposed to deeply sensitizing, live-in experiences—experiences that forced at least a temporary shift in daily routine or in
life style—have seemed to be significantly more open to change and
difference, significantly more accepting of cultural and behavioral

diversity. While there is not yet definitive information for any duration, one tends to trust the professional judgment of a number of leaders of such programs that they, too, have perceived important progress among teachers so exposed.

One evaluation of 61 institutes of teachers of "disadvantaged" youth was conducted by Project Aware through the Bank Street College of Education in New York City. (8) Perhaps the most significant finding was that there was a great deal more emphasis in those institutes upon insight into the life styles of the poor than upon new instructional procedures. That speaks rather clearly, it seems, about the understanding of the institute leaders concerning what is needed among teachers of the poor.

What about a preparation program for all teachers-to-be that establishes a designated group of, say, sixty students teamed together with four faculty members and living close to each other, and close to (or on) the campus for the second two years of college life. The faculty could be from the disciplines of: (1) psychology or educational psychology (with, one hopes, some public educational experience), (2) sociology and/or philosophy (again, with public school exposure), (3) history and/or political science (with the same conditions), and (4) one current public school teacher, either secondary or elementary. Other faculty would be involved as specialists, consultants, resource people, etc., for students concentrating in various subjects—art, music, literature, journalism, biology. . . .

The core of professors would do more than offer isolated classes in their specialty areas. They would *be there* for the learners, develop a closeness of feeling with them, release the learners' very real but often stifled creativity. The teachers-to-be would be obliged to take charge of their own direction—they would be self-propelling individuals; their evaluation would come from within, dictated by the goals they had set for themselves. Intercourse among themselves would make confidence in expression grow and promote true sharing of ideas. Learning and the business of becoming a dedicated teacher would be an ongoing, continual process, one which would be a part of dinner, lunch, and the close-time between roommates just before going to sleep. Swapping feelings with an experienced leader would add to the dynamic reexamination of the ideas of both.

And, perhaps most significantly, the team of faculty or leaders would have a personal stake in their sixty people. Each team going through a college or university would have its unique character and approach. And eventually, students might learn to choose their teams by the atmosphere each one creates, or the emphases the students come to recognize and to anticipate.

The overall effect of the live-in institute would be a kind of supportive, interacting, and highly personalized two years, where students who are becoming teachers would devote at least as much time in any given day to their profession as teachers who are in the schools find they must. A live-in type of institute as the model for teacher preparation might overcome the shortcomings of: (1) the fifty-minute, three-day-a-week course, (2) the alienation that students in college feel from each other and from their professors, (3) the chopped-up, mincemeat approach to the various areas of subject matter, (4) the text book, ivory-tower, irrelevant kinds of experiences students are forced into, and (5) the overemphasis upon the stultifying, the rote memorizing, the drill, the impersonal.

But living in for two years does not guarantee that anything meaningful would occur. Its description requires attention to specific activities and the general options in the structure of the program if it is to be a truly meaningful alternative to present conditions.

On-Site Experiences

Sensitive teachers must be created at least partly by real-life experiences which combine the theoretical with the practical and immediate. Teachers of powerless children need to understand rather early in their education the characteristics of powerlessness: what it feels like to be a "different" child and to confront the mysterious world of abstractions and school-type activities. Our new teachers need to argue about *how* children learn at the same time that they *see* children learn. More and more this means that classes for prospective teachers will need to be conducted directly at a public school.

In the institute approach to teacher preparation, such an on-site arrangement could be established through the public school member of the team. It might very well be that young apprentice teachers will find themselves getting a lot more involved with the children than they expect, especially if they spend ever greater amounts of actual time at a school. They could be actively helping teachers and children from the first day of their first exposure to their educational institute. And with the kind of sensitivity that the new live-in structure will begin to uncover, most teachers-to-be could be uniquely helpful in uplifting and enhancing culturally diverse and culturally shamed children.

One short-term teacher institute conducted in 1967 over the summer months included a one-week live-in in a black ghetto for all the teachers in the program. Some of the teachers were shocked at the conditions they were exposed to, some among them gave up before the week was out and moved to a modern, all-electric motel nearby.

Several tolerated the cultural diversity, some actually enjoyed it, but few could tolerate the elements of poverty they confronted. The experience was, after all, the single most powerful influence of the entire summer's program in sensitizing the teachers to the life styles of the children they teach. It is likely that a similar sensitization would occur among young teachers-to-be were they also exposed at an early stage in their program to the real and varied worlds of our urban centers.

On-site experiences have the added benefits of providing for immediate reaction to problems uncovered. A teacher might experience a vital encounter with a child or a class of children at ten o'clock in the morning in Room 10; and at eleven o'clock she might be with 12 other learners in Room 8, arguing and debating the lessons to be learned. But another factor must be allowed for in a total experience in teacher education. Sensitivity and the development of human awareness should not be left to chance, even if an on-site program is initiated. Actual structured encounter situations—times set aside during an institute day or week—are needed for the systematic approach to personality expansion.

There is an explosion of encounter groups in some areas of the country. Industry long ago got excited about T-groups for their management and supervising personnel. Encounter groups, confrontation groups, and sensitivity groups blanket California, at colleges and universities, mental health clinics, mountain and sea-coast retreats. Institutions such as Synanon, originally started as a supportive, new-life approach to help drug users, established their unique forms of confrontation situations. In Watts, a group of blacks initiated Operation Bootstrap, a self-help agency that included a weekly encounter situation; there, young black people took on white visitors to the ghetto, many of them students, and used a kind of shock technique to coerce them into examining their feelings.

The Encounter Group

At most teacher-education institutions, such encounter situations are reserved for graduate students, and often only for those graduate students who are studying psychology or counselor education. Occasionally, the on-campus counseling center will conduct regular groups, but these usually have the connotation of therapy, and many students avoid them. Institutions of higher learning admit the usefulness of the sensitizing group experience only for specific students.

In teacher-education, there is some evidence—though it is not conclusive—that such encounter situations have impact on teacher sensitivity. Carr, Keislar, and Edwards recently conducted a study to ascertain the value of encounter-group experience for a teacher-preparation curriculum. Their major hypothesis was that compared with students in a task-oriented experience students in the group experience for one academic quarter would show increased appreciation for values involved in personal and social development in relation to academic achievement. The study showed that the participants in the group approach rated their experience highly favorably; there was strong evidence that "dramatic changes" in personality were also accomplished. (1)

In another study, Harry (5) examined 81 student teachers exposed to T-group experiences for 75 minutes a week for seven weeks. A follow-up questionnaire showed that a majority of the participants felt that the T-group exposure had been beneficial for personal growth, for relations with their students, their cooperating teachers, and other people.

Indeed, Rogers, in *Freedom to Learn,* (16) his first full-length venture into the teaching-learning area, devotes significant space to the renewal and growth of an entire school system through the use of encounter group experiences. The notion of "vertical grouping" has been suggested as a way of opening up communication among all segments of an academic community; that is, superintendent, board members, principals, teachers, scholarship students, and school drop-outs, all involved in the same group situation. More is being researched and written each day on the uses of small group encounters in teaching and other helping relationships. (7, 9, 11, 14, 18, 20, 23)

Well, why all these movements toward group interaction for teachers-to-be? In fact, why the emphasis on such exposure for all teachers? (There is such a move to have in-service sensitivity groups for on-the-job teachers.) In a small desert-community elementary-school district, the superintendent, six principals, and two administrative aides went off to the mountains for a three-day retreat in the late spring. They engaged in some soul-searching and examined some rather tricky relationship barriers which had been impeding cooperation among schools. When they returned, the suggestion was made to them that each school, with all its teachers, might benefit from just such a going away, planning, and thinking time. The idea was that each school is an entity in itself, with its peculiar needs and student populations. Often the teachers have little communication with each other and a poor sense of common purpose, become alienated from each other, and ultimately work at cross-purposes with each other. The primary grade teachers, because of their hours, often do not ever see the upper grade teachers. Small talk over coffee or at recess seldom confronts the critical problems of making the educational program relevant to the students.

Instead of the "orientation" meetings the week before school starts, it was suggested that a long weekend (or week, if funds allowed) away somewhere might prove exciting, enjoyable, and useful as well. Perhaps an outside group initiator could be there as a guide, to help to start some intense and lengthy encounter situations which might result in creating a real operating team in which each member had some kind of warmth and respect for the others, understood that there was a mutuality of purpose for the institution, and, once sensitized to other members, could not help but have greater sensitivity for the children.

For sensitizing individuals toward more effective institutional operations, the encounter group appears quite plausible. What about as an instrument in the education of new teachers, prior to their joining any specific team or school? What expansive or enhancing effect can such an experience have on any given young recruit?

Aside from the growing research evidence, a portion of which was cited above, there are some intuitive evidence and some extrapolated reactions from others outside of education about the values of their encounter exposures. Carl Rogers has reported the effects of encounter group experiences he had either organized or conducted with people of all ages and backgrounds. Rogers sent out over 425 follow-up questionnaires in the course of a year, ranging from two to twelve months after the conclusion of the groups. Only two individuals felt that the experience had changed their behavior in ways they did not like. Fifteen percent believed it had made no perceptible change in their behavior. Sixteen percent felt that, while a change in behavior had occurred, it was transitory or had left only a minimal positive residue. Sixty-five percent felt that it had made an ongoing positive difference in their behavior, with a few believing that it had made some concomitant negative changes. (17) But the weighting is clearly and heavily positive, and against doubts about the benefits of intensive group experiences.

Robeck and Wilson studied the usefulness of encounter-grouping when the group consisted of three teams of principals, primary teachers, and auxiliary persons, all from schools with high concentrations of "disadvantaged" children. Each subgroup of three was from the same school so that, in effect, a "team" was being sensitized. For six weeks, each group met for one and one-half hours daily. Through several controlled assessments, the following major conclusion was cited: sensitizing experiences can be focused on particular areas of personal interaction and can have salutary effects on personal relations within a school. (13) Distinctive in the study is its attempt (apparently successful) to place a quantified evaluation upon subjective change in adults.

One radical but tantalizing experiment that I would like to challenge any school district to attempt is to establish encounter groups between a school's teachers and sets of parents from their classrooms. What remarkable communication could result from, say, two or three teachers sitting-in regularly with a dozen parents and experiencing each other's life perceptions! There is, unfortunately, no citable research to substantiate belief in the value of such encounters, since they have rarely been tried. There are, however, in work in all areas of social science numerous implications of the promise in just such an interaction.

Sensitivity experiences are no longer considered mysterious attempts to invade the privacy of the psyche; they are not, as one disoriented, reactionary group recently proclaimed, attack sessions in which one's individuality is sacrificed to the will of the group.

One of the most succinct statements about the purpose of the sensitivity group that has appeared was, interestingly enough, one of the earliest ones made, in 1962:

Our version of sensitivity training increasingly concerns itself with the strengthening of the individual in his desires to experience people and events more fully, to know himself more intimately and accurately, to find a more significant meaning for his life, and to initiate or sustain a process of individual growth toward ever-increasing personal adequacy. (22)

Despite the logical fallacy of using the word "training" with a notion of human personality sensitization, with such a definition in front of every school administrator and every school of education dean, it seems rather unlikely that much objection could still be voiced about the usefulness of encounter groups for teachers or teachers-to-be.

One final commentary seems to point, indirectly, to the enormous need for sensitive teachers and teacher educators. A middle-aged black woman, finally given a chance to finish her college education under an Educational Opportunities Program, was counseled toward classes taught by exceptionally humane and sensitive professors. The aim was to have her first experience back at school be with faculty who had some feel for the dilemma of the black in white America. She wrote the following evaluation of her first semester's experience:

_____ was one of the finest people I have met, so unusual from most instructors who hold his position in other classes I have taken.

_____ was very good, she has a unique and positive way of criticizing or saying to one, "you didn't do so well."

_____ was a fine man; this was a course I really enjoyed; I don't think I was penalized for speaking out.

I have had about thirty-six college instructors before I came to this college, and never before have I felt so free and not afraid to speak out for fear of being penalized. Some professors are alright they think, but will not accept all points of view from students. I attended a history class at a junior college ten years ago. Only one person in that class spoke to me during the whole six weeks session. I, for one, can appreciate the attitude of change among students and professors. I could describe the semester at _____ as one of the finest experiences I have ever had.

This student, formerly marginal in grades and motivation, received three B's and two A's for her semester's work. It is interesting that she interprets her experience as evidence of a "change among students and professors." One wonders how general that change has been.

Government literature these days talks about the "target" group, or the people any given program is supposed to reach. With some sarcasm, we use that term to represent the population any given teacher will be prepared to serve. Since each school is set in its own miniculture, it seems imperative that teachers expecting to teach the culturally different have some exposure during their professional preparation to the particular group they will encounter. It is part of the total experience of becoming an effective facilitator.

Understanding the "Target" Population

Part of the curricular preparation of teachers of the powerless should be an intensive exposure to the sociological and psychological aspects of their condition. A series of dynamic experiences, where teachers-to-be engage in field work in the community and then gather together at community centers to theorize and synthesize, would be significant and relevant. Professors may have to learn to conduct classes at the local "Joint Ventures" project house, or the neighborhood "Half-way House," or the barrio pool hall, or the Boys Club recreation room. . . .

Well-prepared facilitators of child learning will need some deep insight into the forces that shape and control the poor and enforce powerlessness among them. A few such insights are presented here as examples of the complexity of the task of understanding children of diversity. Such insights, I feel, can only be appropriated, understood, and fully utilized through direct exposure and encounter. . . .

For example, the phenomenon of self-hate among black children is a tragic and very real fact of life.* That it stems in part from the constant and reinforcing impact of the dominant culture's insensitivity

---

* In a questionnaire filled out by 120 Harlem elementary school children, and reported by Trubowitz, (21) most of the Negro children felt that white children would not want to go to school with them; they also felt that white children perceived them as less interested in school and less intelligent than the whites. And in a New England city an 8-year-old black girl wished for two things from Santa Claus: that she be happy and that she be white.

should not be ignored in our teacher-preparation curriculum. The shame that some parents feel from being on welfare is a powerful force in their desire or ability to relate to the middle-class teacher.

The instability of the school population must be considered. Poor housing and the search for work make for highly transient family units. It is not unusual for up to one-third of all children in a center-city school to transfer out in any given year. Teachers need to be aware of this fact of life about ghetto schooling and the relative insecurity of the student population.

Powerless parents often have a distorted and self-demeaning awe of their children's teachers. One Chicano college student leader related this story:

My neighbor's little seven-year-old kept asking the teacher in Spanish if he could go to "el baño." The Anglo teacher naturally didn't understand him, so he finally ran out the door and did it out in the dirt. She got mad and sent him to the principal who gave him two swats and told him to behave and do what his teacher said. When the child got home and told his father what the principal had swatted him for, the father told him that he was wrong and that he had better show more respect for his teacher. Teachers and principals don't spank children for wanting to go to the bathroom.

So the powerless sink deeper into self-despair, self-blame, and a reinforced sense of their own ineptitude. How can sensitive facilitators function to intercept and to inhibit the ripening of such damaging self-images?

A student teacher told the following anecdote:

I was tutoring a young Chicano boy from the third grade. His mother talks only Spanish and his father a little English. The regular teacher asked me to spend some time with Celestino alone. I wanted so much to help him, but he would hardly react to me. I told him I would go to the library and get some books for him and I asked what kind he would like. I asked him, "cowboys, dogs, trees, or what?" And all he did was repeat back to me softly and respectfully the last thing I said, "trees." He's so damned respectful and meek, I just don't know how to get to him.

What is there in Celestino's life experience that has influenced that respect and subordination? What does the Chicano family expect of him in his relationship with his teachers? And most critically, what *might* have happened if even one of Celestino's teachers in public school could have spoken and understood Spanish?

These few examples illustrate the complexity of the belief systems and living styles of the culturally different and the powerless, and point up the need for intense, on-the-scene interactional exposure as a regular facet of the curriculum of teacher preparation. There appears to be a growing awareness of the *need* for intense and comprehensive appreciation of the cultural styles of the "target" population. There also appears to be evidence that some teacher-preparation institutions are willing to take the massive steps that will remove their programs from the category of *experimental*.

One way that has been tried which recognized such a need was a mid-1960s program at Fordham University. (12) As part of the curricular experience of teachers-to-be, each student spent a semester of volunteer work as a community service aide and a semester of paid service as a school aide during his junior year of college. In his senior year, each student served as an assistant teacher to a specially selected classroom teacher for three hours a day for the full year. Part of his task was to assume increasing responsibility for tutoring individuals and for teaching small groups and eventually the whole class. For his work, he was paid 25 percent of the annual salary of a beginning teacher. And then as a graduate student, in his fifth year, he was to become an intern teacher, carry one-half the load of the regular teacher at one-half the salary. This program represented a positive attempt to bring real life into the teacher-preparation program, and also to offer immediate manpower assistance to the schools which needed it most.

Other fruitful experiments in integrating on-the-job, culturally expansive experiences with the teacher-preparation curriculum have been conducted at Syracuse University through their Urban Education Program, (10) and as part of the student-intern team-teaching programs in Pittsburgh, Pennsylvania. (19)

To this point, we have focused upon the myriad ways in which becoming a facilitator can and must be a total, all-absorbing kind of exposure. Let us now examine ways in which a true facilitator can relate to and enhance the powerless youngsters he encounters.

Most new teachers who confront their classes of ghetto children for the first time are dreadfully concerned about discipline. Books which purport to treat the problems of educating the "disadvantaged" pay elaborate attention to the expressed concerns of urban teachers about the unruly nature of their students. Formulae are offered showing ways to structure one's classroom for maximum interaction while at the same time maintaining control and order. Even writings which, in other ways, show unusual perceptiveness about the life

Facilitating Learning among the Powerless

Discipline and Control

styles and psychological patterns of the culturally different of our country fall into the trap of symptom-treating. That is, while there is recognition of the validity of "discovery" approaches to learning and of the impact of the learner's motivation and perceptual world upon the curriculum, there is still the rather dissonant echo of teacher-centeredness that seems to confuse thinking, and to offer structural "how to's" for discipline and control. Thus, for example, one book examines with deep insight the needs and the mountainous despair of the powerless, but still promotes a section instructing the teacher to combine "strength with sensitivity" when disciplining his students. (2) Unfortunately, the latter appears to miss the point; it is the children, powerless as they are, who need the strength.

We must strive, however, to release, not control, the feelings of our students. The critical factor in discipline is that order grows out of internalizing a value or a belief; order cannot be imposed from the outside. Whitney Young, of the Urban League, speaking in 1969 to a conference of counselors and teachers, expressed such an idea in a rather succinct and incisive way: "Let us stop trying to make a god out of order. Let us make a god out of justice and we will, in fact, have order." (24)

Classroom discipline is inextricably linked to motivation: Children who are excited about their activities are too busy to disrupt; children who are caught up in their work apply their own order and discipline. Focusing on controlling the disruption detracts from focusing on ways to excite the learners. When children who have been powerless get turned on to learning, the emergence of curiosity and pride and power overcomes the narrow notion of control; rather, the channeling of the exuberance for learning becomes the teacher's primary challenge.

I was once fortunate enough to learn the lesson of internal discipline in an easy way. As teacher of an "X" group (bright youngsters) of tenth graders in an English class some years ago, I discovered early in the semester that these particular boys and girls were highly and deeply motivated for learning. The class read *Julius Caesar,* learned some of the speeches and acted them out; read *Les Miserables* and saw its Hollywood film version; read and discussed numerous essays, short stories, and poems; and wrote creatively in whatever form they desired. The "set" curriculum was easily covered two weeks before the semester was over, and the class asked to read *The Old Man and the Sea,* by Hemingway. A new set of that book had just arrived, and despite the English department chairman's admonition that it was not scheduled to be read until the eleventh grade, our class had its way. The fascinating and instructive aspect of that semester was that there was *never* a disciplinary problem. When occasionally a student or two got distracted, bored, or irritated, or began to bother the others in the class, the class turned to them and asked them to "knock it off." It was uncanny how the class itself took away from the teacher any need to discipline its members; it was as if the common purpose of the class were centered on learning, and that purpose had become contagious. There is every evidence that, had I tried to impose a discipline or a control when *I* deemed it necessary, it might totally have missed the time when the students felt it necessary. *They* were the learners, it was *their* class, *they* knew when they were disturbed or irritated by certain behavior, or when, at other times, it added to the climate of stimulation and curiosity.

While certainly the youngsters described above were highly charged, capable, and self-disciplined, the really critical issue is whether their excitement and curiosity maintained their self-discipline, or whether their discipline is what added to their enthusiasm about learning. Our present convictions lean toward the former hypothesis. And if that is indeed so, then getting turned on to learning, not only for the acknowledged right student but for the alienated and the defeated as well, carries with it its own form of self-discipline and control.

I wrote earlier about the need for a facilitator to come across to his learners as really caring, as prizing them highly as unique and capable people, in order to provide what is a most unusual and powerful incentive. It is almost as if a child of poverty, feeling desolate and inferior, looks upon the middle-class, all-powerful teacher as a confusing and demanding god. The sense of worthlessness pervades the personality and interferes with the motivation to know, "to strive, to seek, to find. . . ."

Caring as a Means of Motivating

Suddenly one of the gods communicates in his manner, his speech, his bearing, his total personality, "I really care for you—you are a remarkable and valuable child—and I believe in you and your desire to know and to understand." A timid child dares to try, and Lo! he is not judged. It is as if the child reasons to himself, "I am not much. This world is not mine. It is too confusing and I am different. But . . . if *he* really likes me, maybe I *am* alright. Maybe there *is* something about me if *he* can like me. . . ."

One is regularly reminded in book and conversation that "love is not enough," and that caring for the child cannot alone lift him from academic inferiority. Of course not: But it would seem that deep and honest caring is necessary as a prerequisite to any other strategy that may be considered. But one brief caution seems necessary. A pretense of caring "because it is the thing to do" will be perceived by the learner

as phony. It is sad if a teacher cannot truly prize his students—but
if he cannot, then possibly he should not try to place himself in a helping relationship to them. His attitude will do more damage than any
of his expertise as a structurer of learning situations can overcome.
Again, we are told that a teacher cannot like all his students; after
all, he is only human. And a fair response is that to the extent that
he does like them, so will he truly be a facilitator for them; to those
whom he cannot like, he will be less helpful, and they will be less free
to learn, less certain about themselves and, ultimately, feel less powerful as human beings.

When one feels good enough about himself, then he is freer to learn
and to try. The curiosity of the powerless is not dead, it is merely
smothered in uncertainty and doubt. The facilitator who is truly sensitive (perhaps made so through interaction in encounter group situations), who is truly saturated in his helping role (perhaps through
intensive live-in teacher-preparation institutes), and who truly prizes
each of his students will be uniquely primed to help release the fettered
power of the poor.

*The Power of
Discovery*

I have already noted that emerging mental health comes to the poor
when a sense of achievement can be felt; that "the poor must do it for
themselves," but that the power structure must give up some of its
power and "let the poor in." Most of the examples referred to curricular, institutional, and societal changes being influenced by the
emerging poor. Presently, mention must be made of the in-classroom
impact upon the powerless of their discovery of their worth and importance.

Because the never-ending polemic between basic and progressive
education has focused upon methodology for the learning structure
for so-called typical students, the argument is futile when it comes to
children of the powerless. The fact is that youngsters who have depressed expectations are not capable of learning through the standard
competitive, externally motivated reward system. Pride and a sense of
confidence just do not seem to grow unless, as with the militants seeking social change, the child in the classroom can do it for himself. And
just as to be effective, the teacher's care must be perceived by the
child, so must the learner perceive himself as having been the instrument of his own learning. A facilitator's role must provide the
structure for students to explore their world, to discover for themselves the knowledge they seek, to become aware of their own self-
made discovery, and to grow in power through this awareness.

Forward-looking educators have called such self-activity *discovery
learning*. It is also widely described as the *inductive approach* to

learning. Powerless youngsters who discover for themselves some hidden and elusive secret, who have worked towards a sought-after insight, and who are undeniably aware of their activity in that discovery, have stored up fuel for the winter. They have been touched with their first taste of power—the power that comes from the knowledge that "I can do it." Guilford has studied its effects on the learner's ability to transfer to new kinds of learning and found them favorable. (4)

The poor have been judged so long that they have never gained the ability to evaluate themselves. We have already scored the American notion of externally imposed, harsh evaluation in our schools. It should suffice here to point out briefly the relationship between a personal, intrinsic locus of evaluation, and the emergence of power among the poor.

The Power of Self-Evaluation

Constant external evaluation, whether examined from a humanistic or a behavioristic viewpoint, conditions the recipient to rely only upon that kind of evaluation. When a mother makes all the decisions for her (powerless) child, he does not learn how to make decisions for himself. The poor have had their decisions made for them, and they have remained powerless and unable to move on their own.

As the poor begin to evaluate themselves, they will begin to create new criteria for excellence and for achievement. (Outside the formal classroom it takes the form, for example, of "black is beautiful," a deliberate attempt at positive self-evaluation.) Judging themselves positively on their own criteria, they will begin to feel good about what they *can* do within their own frame of reference. They will (and do) buoy each other up and offer each other pride and dignity and power. They will (and have started to) form their own subcultural *cooperacy.* A poor child of tomorrow must be able to say, "I have looked at myself and I find myself good and capable. I have looked at myself and I find myself different but beautiful. I have looked *hard* at myself and I find more that is one with my brothers than at odds. I am good and I can make it—and *it* cannot be defined by harsh and judgmental others. *It* can only be defined by me and my awareness of myself and my own goals."

A facilitator who is sensitive can relate to his children in such a way that they begin to evaluate themselves and to establish personal criteria of excellence. A facilitator who cares deeply for his children will not place each of their decisions under *his* scrutiny; he will, rather, offer his students the chance to discover that their own estimates of self-need and of self-achievement have strength and validity. And from this locus of evaluation will come increased power to deal with the next and the next and the next emergent decision. There is growing research evidence to show that teachers who see their purpose as one of *freeing* rather than *controlling* students are perceived by their students as effective teachers. (3, 6)

Facilitating through Student Encounters

Student encounter groups, even when led by the regular teacher, have begun to show promise as instruments of growth and creative release for individuals and for entire classes. Some teachers have described to me how they have set aside a two-hour block of time every week with their young children and joined them in expressing feelings about their week, their friends, their studies, each other, the teacher. . . . When the teacher joins in, becomes one of the group, and really reaches into his affective world, there is a kind of human quality that comes across to his students. It becomes contagious, and they too feel free to be honest and to drop their facades.

Other teachers, after having exposure to deeply sensitizing group experiences, have tried to organize groups in their schools (often over the opposition of the principal or other administrators). Some have described how they have tried sack lunch, noontime groups (and have found the time too limited), after-school groups (and have found conflicts with parents or jobs or other duties), or even conference-period groups (and have found other teachers resentful that children leave their classes).

In one remarkably successful group program, two teacher-counselors in a rather solidly middle-class high school in the Far West formed small discussion groups for students who were using various drugs. They laid down very few restrictions, but one of them was that no one could be on drugs in any way while a member of the group. The group met at least one evening a week at the home of one of the counselors. The characteristic mood of the group was unusually accepting and open and caring; the two counselors (one black, the other white) showed sincere interest and affection for each student. The word-of-mouth impact of the group was so powerful on all segments of the campus that several new leaders were initiated and new groups started; other schools and districts, some of them with high populations of poverty youngsters, contacted the founders to be consultants in initiating programs for them. It has obviously caught on as a facilitating device for knitting together alienated young people.

In another situation with which I was personally involved, a group of "disruptive" fourth-grade youngsters was referred for special action to curb their hostilities and classroom behavior. Nine of us met as a group for 14 consecutive weeks, for only one hour each week. The activity within the group ranged among conversation, drawing and coloring, and acting out strong and varied feelings—by, for example, climbing onto my lap or by sometimes poking at or wrestling with each other.

All the children in the group were asked to fill out a short questionnaire at the first meeting and were later reassessed to see if after the group experience any of the self-perceptions were different. (A control group, not counseled, made up of "conforming, good kids" was also assessed to use as a comparison.) Perhaps the most interesting findings in this small study were that (1) the counseled students found themselves getting into significantly fewer fights in school after the counseling than before—before counseling they had seen themselves fighting much more than the control group saw themselves fighting; (2) after counseling, the counseled students expressed themselves significantly more candidly than they did before; for example, after counseling, four of the eight admitted getting into arguments at home "almost always," while before counseling, only one had so declared; the same was true with the statement, "I like my teacher," where six counseled students cited "almost never" after counseling, while only one in that group had so declared prior to counseling; interestingly, in the control group, seven of the eight cited "almost always" on that statement.

But the overall importance of this group experience was that in the semester following, *not one* of the children in the group was referred by any teacher to the principal for special help. And perhaps of particular significance is that the group experience seemed instrumental in both releasing and channeling the camouflaged feelings of the members. They appeared to become more aware of the impact their behavior had been having on others, and simultaneously they seemed to become more honestly expressive.

It is the contention here—and more and more evidence seems to indicate some justification for the belief—that with all students, and particularly with the powerless, an opportunity to regularly express their feelings about their school exposures acts as a powerful facilitating device in releasing their inhibitions about learning. What impedes learning among the poor has not been their dullness or their lassitude; it has been their *feelings* about themselves that they cannot learn—in a word, it has been their powerlessness.

Both promising and exhilarating are the seeming advances some of our teachers-to-be have made toward becoming true understanders and true facilitators of the poor. In a class for prospective teachers, with whom I have been associated, over thirty young people participated in a semester-long program in barrio and ghetto schools in a large city on the West Coast. There was no way to know what impact such experiences were having on the young students, although they seemed to be exuberant and deeply involved in their work. In order to assess some of their feelings and perceptions, the following question was asked to which the response was made in writing: "Cite examples and explain why ghetto education has been largely irrelevant to minority students." The statements below, extremely critical of existing situations, indicate a certain remarkable insight into the needs of the culturally different.

A New Hope: Some Perceptions of Teachers-to-Be

In response to the question posed above, the following selected excerpts represent the tone of the answers:

A junior woman, art major, wrote:

The educational material is geared toward the white middle class. The contribution of minority peoples to the growth of this country is virtually ignored. White-blacks are mentioned, but not black-blacks. . . . Black schools are run by whites with the ever-present attitude, "we know better for you than you do." The school promotes the status quo, and divergence in peoples is neither explored nor accepted.

A junior woman, English major, wrote:

In the ghetto, the subject matter must be relevant. The teachers themselves must be in a sense relevant. They must be familiar with life in a ghetto if they are to, first, understand the problems and areas of difficulty these children will have in learning, and then, second, create meaningful learning situations for them.

A senior woman, sociology major, wrote:

If we consider school as a place where people learn to read and write, then ghetto schools have failed, because a large percentage of the children in them cannot read and write. . . . If schools are also for making responsive, responsible adults, then the schools in the ghetto have failed two-fold. Children must believe that they are worthwhile persons in order to grow up to feel that way. . . . To give ghetto children *Dick and Jane Run with Spot* is pure hogwash. And to expect them to come in with the values held by their teachers, values of promptness, neatness, orderliness, obedience, etc., is to make them more turned off. Black, Mexican-American, and Indian children rarely see adults like themselves as anything worth respecting. Therefore, ghetto teachers must themselves come from the ghetto, so that the children can identify with them and develop the admirable qualities they find in the people they respect.

A senior woman, history major, wrote:

Ghetto children are subject to the teaching skills of people who are ill-equipped and experienced. The novice teacher in her white Mustang from the West Side cannot (and moreover does not) even attempt to relate to the students. I really get sick talking ʾɔ my friends who are teaching in ghetto areas—they simply say the kids won't listen, and give up.

A junior man, physical education major, wrote:

At _____ Junior High in the ghetto the teachers don't give a damn about the welfare of the students and consequently it reflects in their teaching. Exercises are conducted on a mass basis with one teacher (or sometimes a loudspeaker) leading a group of 120 students. In my college classes I learned that individuality should be stressed when teaching physical education. No such thing is being done at _____ Junior High. When the instructor tells the class they will run the whole period, this does nothing to shed light on why, or what benefit the running will have on the students' bodies. . . .

A junior woman (black), speech major, wrote:

Many minority groups' environments are not designed for an education: crowded conditions, living near the train tracks, rats, roaches, a lack of food, and no transportation. Ghetto education is irrelevant because the students have a lack of motivation and of confidence in themselves to compete with the "better half" of our society.

A junior man, anthropology major, wrote:

From the time they enter school until they leave, ghetto children are engaged in a kind of contest. They are not learning and, what is worse, they are being forced to distrust learning (formal and even their own) by the actual methods designed to instill knowledge. Is it relevant for the black ghetto child to be concerned with Middle English poetry, suburbia's life style, and space development, to the exclusion of his own personal being? It is nonsensical that white, middle-class America is so culturally narrow and unaccepting that different culture patterns are automatically viewed as inferior.

A junior woman, sociology major, wrote:

The information the children receive doesn't apply to their world and it causes their self-concepts to crumble. The small children read how Dick and Jane live in nice neighborhoods where the mailman always pats them on the head and the mother always has milk and cookies waiting for them when they get home. The ghetto children read this garbage that doesn't apply to them and then go home to their over-crowded tenements where the mailman doesn't give a damn about them and they are lucky if they get a filling dinner, let alone an afternoon snack.

A senior woman, history major, wrote:

Until recently, and [the change] has not begun to occur on any significant scale, ghetto children had white American history forced on them. They were told they had to respect Washington and Jefferson, men who held their great grandparents in chains. They were given no historical figures, no literary idols, no successful black examples of what they could aspire to be. English classes still teach minority students to be ashamed of their dialects, dialects which are more rich and commanding than standard English in a lot of cases.

A senior woman, drama major, wrote:

Of all the ghetto people, the black man is the easiest example for me to cite because there has been so much controversy about his predicament. Bill Cosby had a very good documentary on Black America in which he pointed out how the black man was always shown in movies as less than average; the wide-eyed, easily scared, slow-moving idiot who was extremely grateful for any kindness by the superior white man . . . It is not a healthy society which causes to be taught to black children that "Black is Beautiful." They should be born and raised with this pride in themselves.

This handful of representative statements contains one rather interesting characteristic. The themes or motifs seem to reflect, if not systematically, almost all the salient arguments expressed in this writing. As we summarize those themes, we are also summarizing our own several positions: The contributions of minorities to the development of this country have been relatively ignored; schools representing the status quo have dominated; there is a relentless need for curricular relevancy; there is also a need for teacher relevancy and sensitivity; there has been a failure of schools to enhance the children who come from poverty; narrow cultural demands and expectations have been made of children who may be different; there has been a lack of role models of the same ethnic or cultural backgrounds for powerless children to encounter; the do-good characteristics of the young, middle-class teacher, and her rapid disillusionment, have pervaded ghetto education; the factory approach and dehumanizing impact of the schools have also been pervasive; a sense of inferiority has been ubiquitous among children of diversity; the humiliation that oppresses those who *cannot* and *have not,* when they are indoctrinated about children who *can* and *have,* has overpowered some children; false perspectives of history have inculcated all children with the myth of the American way; a degradation has accompanied language and speech variations; and an overreaction that attempts to create pride and power through solidarity, disdain, a reshuffling of goals, and a building of personal perspectives, has exploded in fury and anger.

Some teachers-to-be show a sensitivity which engenders profound hope about tomorrow; show promise of an awareness which has portent for the future of education; and appear to be on their way to becoming open, creative, and releasing facilitators.

The perceptions of some of the people who are in the process of becoming teachers represent a new hope for the powerless. As John Collier has written of "the long hope" for the Indians of America, so must "the new hope" be expressed for all of the people of poverty in our country. That new hope rests with the creation and continued development of a new colony of facilitators who understand and appreciate the magnificence of human diversity. That new hope rests with a more humanizing, less stultifying, less structured experience of professional preparation for people who are to be helpers. And that new hope rests with the awareness that a teacher is a releaser, not a controller, an initiator not a manipulator.

True facilitators must understand the nature of discovery and must tolerate differences in pacing, in curiosity, in methodology; they must offer the child an unconditional chance to try for himself, and they must relinquish the role of judge and evaluator. When the *child* achieves and knows it, senses his control, and feels his power, he is on his way to vigorous and rewarding encounters with life.

While teachers are largely in-the-school employees, when working with children of differing life styles they must reach for more imaginative approaches. To be relevant, a teacher must be *in* and *of* and often *for* the community. Chapter 9 will consider the intricacies of community activity for tomorrow's facilitator.

Notes   1. Carr, Genevieve, Evan R. Keislar, and Joseph Edwards. "Encounter Groups in Teacher Preparation." A paper presented at the California Educational Research Assoc. Conference, Los Angeles, California, March 5, 1969.

2. Fantini, Mario D., and Gerald Weinstein. *The Disadvantaged: Challenge to Education*. New York: Harper, 1968.

3. Gooding, C. T. "An Observational Analysis of the Perceptual Organization of Effective Teachers." Unpublished Ed.D. Dissertation, Gainesville: University of Florida, 1964.

4. Guilford, J. P. "Factors that Aid and Hinder Creativity," in Don E. Hamachek, editor, *Human Dynamics in Psychology and Education*. Boston: Allyn and Bacon, 1968, pp. 156–172.

5. Harry, Shizuko N. "Student Teachers and T-Groups." Unpublished paper, Univ. of Utah, 1966.

6. Hildman, C. K. "A Projective Analysis of the Perceptual Organization of Effective Teachers." Unpublished Ed.D. Dissertation, Gainesville: Univ. of Florida, 1966.

7. Joyce, B. *et al.* "Sensitivity Training for Teachers: An Experiment." *Journal of Teacher Education,* 20: 75–83. Spring 1969.

8. Klopf, Gordon J., and Gorda W. Bowman. *Teacher Education in a Social Context*. New York: Mental Health Materials Center, 1966.

9. Lee, W.S. "Human Relations Training for Teachers: The Effectiveness of Sensitivity Training." *California Journal of Educational Research.* 21:28–34, January 1970.

10. Milner, Ernest J. "Preparing Teachers for Urban Schools: The Syracuse Program." Clearinghouse on Urban Teacher Education Report, Vol. 2, No. 1, Spring 1966.

11. Preuss, William J. "The Initiation and Evaluation of a Human Relations Program Conducted by Teacher Training Students in an Elementary School" Final Report. Washington, D.C.: U.S. Department of Health, Education, and Welfare, Office of Education, Bureau of Research, June 1969.

12. Rivlin, Harry N. *Teachers for Our Big City Schools*. New York: Anti-Defamation League of B'nai B'rith, 1964–1965.

13. Robeck, Mildred C., and John A. R. Wilson. "Toward a Quantified Evaluation of Sensitivity Change." A paper presented at the Calif. Educational Research Assoc. Conference, Los Angeles, California, March 15, 1969.

14. Roberts, Julian. "Needed Research in Teacher Education—Sensitivity Training and the Process of Change." A paper presented at Educational Research Association of New York State and the New York State Education Department Convocation Albany, November 1967.

15. Rogers, Carl. "The Characteristics of a Helping Relationship," in P. T. Hountras, *Mental Hygiene—A Text of Readings*. Columbus, O.: C. E. Merrill Books, Inc., 1961, pp. 441–459.

16. Rogers, Carl. *Freedom to Learn*. Columbus: C. E. Merrill Books, Inc., 1969.

17. Rogers, Carl. "The Process of the Basic Encounter Group." Unpublished paper at the Western Behavioral Sciences Institute, La Jolla, California, 1966.

18. Sigut, W., and R. Lohr. "Teacher Sensitivity Groups." *Pennsylvania School Journal*. 118: 30. Summer, 1969.

19. Smith, E. Brooks, and Patrick J. Johnson, editors. Report number one: "School College Relationships in Teacher Education: Report of a National Survey of Cooperative Ventures"; and Report number two: "Cooperative Structures in School College Relationships for Teacher Education." Washington, D.C.: American Association of Colleges for Teacher Education, 1964–1965.

20. Strunk, B. B. "Programs in Progress: Sensitivity Training." *School Management*. 13: 58. Summer 1969.

21. Trubowitz, Sidney. *A Handbook for Teaching in the Ghetto School*. Chicago: Quadrangle Books, 1968, p. 69.

22. Wechsler, Irving, Fred Massarik, and Robert Tannenbaum. "Sensitivity Training." Unpublished paper, Los Angeles, California, 1962.

23. Wilson, L. S. "Inservice Training: Lifeline for Integration." *Nation's Schools*. 84: 70–71. October 1969.

24. Young, Whitney. From a speech delivered at the American Personnel and Guidance Association Annual Convention, Las Vegas, Nevada: March 31, 1969.

Chapter Nine

The Teacher and the Community

Statement: We must not get too involved with our students, too personal with them, too caught up in their community or in their lives; if we do we will lose our objectivity.

(*Professor of geography at a West Coast college, 1969*)

Response: It seems to me that in this day, we need to lose a bit of our objectivity and become somewhat more subjective; after all, our students are subjects, not objects.

(*Director of the Educational Opportunities Program at the same college, 1969*)

If teachers who will be encountering powerless children are indeed to be facilitators, they must be aware of the impact they can and do have upon the community, and vice versa.

Most of our teachers live, spend their salaries, and socialize outside their school's service area. What effect does this have upon the children, their parents, and the community at large? How do they view the school, and what can be done to make the school an integral agency of the community?

The parents of the community expect that teachers will learn about the neighborhood and the people in it. One parent expressed the feelings of many when she said: "The people of the community resent those teachers who have bad things to say about the community and never come outside the schools. The parents say to themselves, 'What do these people know about our community? They just drive to school and drive away. What do they know about us?'. . . What we need is someone from the community to work with the parents and the school, someone who knows the people, because the parents are afraid to give their insides to teachers. They will to someone from the community." (4)

The Live-in Teacher

There are many reasons why most teachers do not wish to live near their schools. Some are remnants of an old, puritanical notion that children should not be exposed to their master while he is at rest or leisure; some are hinged to morality, but have assumed a peculiarly administrative quality in that principals tend to caution teachers to go to lounges well away from their youngsters' precincts. Letting one's hair down is something that if seen by students would certainly lessen respect and esteem.

Other teachers have openly stated that their private lives are their own. "Why," they will add, "are teachers expected to devote their entire lives to their students, while other professionals can leave their work at the office?" There is a lingering petulance and a resentment in such a statement (perhaps justified) that teachers are not quite considered *as* professional as the other *true* pros. . . .

Still more teachers have taken a rather strict economic position about their residence. That is, "We have worked hard so that we could afford nice homes in pleasant, green, tranquil communities; we wish the same for our students, and we hope the work we are doing will enable them to achieve a similar situation some day."

By themselves, probably each of the above arguments had some merit, at least at one time. Certainly the teacher conceives that he has served humanity with so much more dedication than most reasonably powerful Americans. Yet the ghettos and the barrios have not disappeared: only a handful of tantalized children have adopted the American dream; and new faces but the same old problems are encountered in the center-city communities.

The very arguments used by middle-class teachers to justify their living where they do live can be used by spokesmen of the poor to support their demands for teachers who are the ethnic and cultural makeup of the children they teach. Such teachers, they argue, *would* devote their entire lives to their students, for their past experiences and their present identities would be the same as their students'. Such teachers would not be afraid of being seen after school by their students, for whom in fact such an encounter would be beneficial. And as for "letting one's hair down," doing so would make the teacher all the more human, real, and acceptable to the community. In the ghetto, it is the oddity (most teachers, in this context, wear that word well) not to socialize on the corner in the late afternoon.

The major criticism of teachers of the poor *by* the poor has been in the area of their true dedication to such "different" youngsters. And in their benevolence, the poor have said, "We do not blame the Anglo teacher for her lack of commitment; after all, they are not *her* people she is teaching." And so, without blame, but with a new singularity of purpose, the poor are saying (as they did in New York City in the fall of 1968), "We want our own teachers, teachers who will understand us and be *for* us, and who will not run away to their house in the hills after servicing the poor little underprivileged kids all day long."

What chance do the poor have to find their schools staffed by teachers of their own ethnic and cultural backgrounds? We can hope, a good chance in the next decade; but small chance in the immediate future. Even the Ocean Hill-Brownsville school board in New York, in the district which launched the now-famous strike of the teachers' union, after firing the existing faculty, restaffed their schools with a majority of white teachers (in a heavily black-population area). So long as credentialing requirements remain as stringent, a massive influx of new teachers from the ghetto areas will be long in coming. This is not to say that others who are noncredentialed cannot work with remarkable impact in the schools—and this will be discussed shortly. But, at least for the present, the licensed teachers who touch the lives of our poor will be largely from the middle class.

And where will they live? There are no indications that the teacher-to-be, sensitive as some seem to be becoming, will trade in his house in suburbia for the relentless squalor of the slums. He will continue to be a daytime teacher. But must he also continue to be solely a schoolroom employee? Perhaps not. . . .

**The Community
Aide and Home
Visits**

In the middle 1960s, teachers were regularly heard to say, "I'm committed to working here all right, but that doesn't mean I have to go walking around in a hostile community. Uh, uh, no home visits for me. If I'm going to see little Althea's mother, she's going to have to come here to the school." No doubt many such fears were based upon very real conditions and rather accurate perceptions by the teachers. But then, the next thought, which certainly has to rankle is: How effective can a teacher (or school) be when the relationship between the institution and the community is admittedly suspicious, antagonistic, restrictive, and basically dishonest? It becomes fairly evident that in the absence of free and open communication there could only have been coercive and inferior education.

The emergence of school aides, such as those described in the Berkeley Plan, (2) may possibly have offered new and exciting options in our schools. Indigenous aides (that is, drawn directly from the community that the school services) provide the children with some sense of identification and a link between the formerly alien, Anglo, and middle-class world of the school, and their day-to-day feeling and sensing world outside. The community aide (also known today as the paraprofessional) not only provides the children with some sense that the schools are relevant to *their* lives, but also provides a communications line to the community. Most teachers *are* middle-class, do not live in the area of the school, come across as mysterious and aloof to the people of the community, and—especially women—*do* have fears about walking through the slums. The community aide can serve as an interpreter in the community, as a companion on home visits and when parents do come to the school, as, in a sense, a protector and a counselor to the teacher. The teacher should find that she can begin to meet parents in *their* setting (although this does not guarantee that her attitude will not be perceived as patronizing or even contemptuous). She should find that the community's activities become events to which she receives invitations (although this does not mean that her presence there will not create a certain discomfort). She should find that her students begin to see her as more believable and more a natural part of their interrelated experiences in the home, community, and school (although this does not guarantee that she will yet be trusted or even understood by her students).

The critical aspect of pairing a member of the larger culture with a member of the subculture surrounding the school, is its potential to open doors and, perhaps for the first time, to touch with some significance the lives of the powerless. In the absence of credentialed teachers who represent the community to be serviced this is the next best plan. The teacher is able to escape the narrowness of the classroom as her arena for engaging in education. And what has been shown by recent studies on the effectiveness of paraprofessionals becomes operational: Extensive technical training is less significant as a positive factor in a helping relationship than is a certain quality of empathy and openness. (1) And people who are *of* the ghetto or the barrio have a rather strong chance to be perceived as emphathetic, open, and caring for the children of their community. And with those qualities operating in a classroom setting, the sense of goodness and of power that the children feel will also act to release their potential as investigators and seekers and learners.

The monetary and logistic problems of providing center-city schools with community aides for the teachers are enormous, as indeed is the potential for bureaucratic mishandling. As a safeguard and to be faithful to democratic principles, it would be useful to approach selection, placement, and implementation with the same new spirit of cooperation discussed earlier. If members of the community are to be workers in the school setting, the community should have some significant role in choosing such members. The community would also seem to be indispensable in helping to define the role of the community aide, her job description, how she will operate in the neighborhood, her relationship to the teacher and to the students. If this were to be implemented, the school system would of course have to agree to give up some of its traditional powers. It is the recurring theme: How much power will the majority be willing to give up in order for the activity and experience of those who are now powerless to have significance and impact?

A final, necessary point about community aides can be made by the following anecdote: A Mexican-American college student recently turned in a case report to me which represented her ten-week participation experience in an elementary school which was 80 percent Mexican-American. The report focused on one fourth-grade child she had been carefully observing and tutoring. The child came from a large family, was not achieving well in school, seemed withdrawn and verbally inhibited. Though seeming to be sensitive to the children and democratic in her approach, the teacher was Anglo and lived miles from the barrio. The college student lived in the barrio, had gone to public school there, and was now in her junior year in college. Her report described her last day at the school, her relationship with the little girl, Lydia, and the encounter that went on. . . .

Lydia: Won't you come back?
Student: Well, I won't be back at this school, but I can see you outside of school.
Lydia: Can I have your phone number?

Student: Sure, and you can call me whenever you like. In fact, maybe you could come over to visit me; I don't live very far from you.
Lydia: Could I really?
Student: Sure!
Lydia: I'll call you and then you can tell me when I can come over.
Student: Okay.

I went home after my classes that afternoon and my mother told me that a little girl named Lydia had called three times. I called her back and she told me her mom had gone shopping with her sisters but she had stayed home with her two baby brothers. She wanted to know when she could come to visit me. It was a great feeling for me to know that this little girl really needed me. And you know, the teacher had let me look in her cumulative records and the anecdotal comments of the teachers from the first through the third grade read like this: (First Grade: Lydia is slow in all academic areas. Refuses to mix with other children. Does not use sentences when talking to teacher.) (Second Grade: Minimal academic progress. Is a withdrawn child. Should be tested for EMR.) (Third Grade: Does not complete work assigned. Is very quiet. Cannot use complete sentences. Seems uninterested in school work.)

It's funny about all those notations, because I feel that Lydia is a very bright child. Maybe it's because I'm Chicano and she feels more at ease with me. . . .

The wisdom in this student's final sentence may not have been fully realized by her. She was a college student, but since she was also from the community, her effect was similar to what a community aide's could be. Had she really reached Lydia? Was Lydia becoming more interested, more alive about her school? Did someone relevant and meaningful and significant to her touch her life *within the school setting?* No miracles occurred, only an identification; no sudden academic discovery, only a relationship. No remarkable advance in achievement, only a very tentative reaching out by a tiny, hungry human being for a communion with another person. Could a community aide in each ghetto and barrio classroom hold any promise for repetitions of Lydia's story? There is mounting evidence to support such a notion.

The Teacher as a Community Aide   The center-city school has been an alien embassy to the people of the community. It does its thing for five or six hours a day and then it bolts its doors and padlocks its fences, while its staff of workers disappear into distant retreats. The community remains . . . and the empty buildings stand solemn, deserted, starkly uninviting, and monuments to grossly misdirected city and human planning.

When the poor attack the structures—when vandals burn or ransack a classroom—it is an attack upon the symbol of the institution. It is an attack upon a hostile, anonymous system which has failed to become personally significant in the lives of the poor. To have to attack the empty and hollow edifice of the system, destroying the very element in the system through which the poor have hope of rising, is grinding evidence of the awesome impact of the powerlessness which grips the poor.

But it need not be that way. The schools *could* become community centers, peopled structures which breathe and pulsate with the life of the neighborhood. The teacher can help this process by becoming an aide in the community. He can help to encourage the active involvement of the adults and young adults from around the school in forming action groups, tutoring groups, political information groups. It is a human and monetary waste to use intricately and aesthetically planned structures only six hours out of every 24.

In most places today, the elusive and distant board must give permission for an approved civic group to use rooms, the cafeteria, the auditorium. It is as if this elected body had suddenly become very possessive and jealous of the physical plants they had found as part of the school system; it is as if the local community, the people whose children are in the schools, had effectively been removed from any influence—except for remote, ballot-box influence—over their own schools.

The schools must be open to the community: recreation, meetings, parties, encounter groups, technical instruction, leadership education, family counseling—what better place is there for all of these activities than in the ubiquitous, strategically located, traditionally empty community schools? The teacher can assume a role of facilitator toward the community as well as toward the children in her class. The practical aspects of scheduling and the limits of human devotion notwithstanding, teachers can contribute (perhaps on a rotating basis with other teachers at the school, or perhaps as a small team available for regular open house, or perhaps as small teams that could visit other community agencies and work with people in *their* surroundings) and can *be there* for the families they are supposed to service.

The critical question becomes: can we ever escape the narrow and traditional role of the teacher as one who has *children come to* him; who has *"a" classroom;* who has narrowly defined *hours when he performs?* Can we begin to expand the potential of a facilitator as a true community worker with unusual skills in human relations; one who is a teacher *in a community,* not a teacher at the school? Can we then look upon his work with a child as *work with a family* and, ultimately, *work with an entire community?* In relation to the potential for a creative, imaginative, and courageous facilitator, the narrow, restrictive concept of the teacher of subject matter alone gets left behind in the dynamic needs of today.

We have intimated that Puerto Rican, Chicano, or black children in our urban slum schools would find a more enhancing school environment if their teachers were members of their own ethnic community. In a larger sense, this is probably true of all people; they are more comfortable with cultural and behavioral consistency and with belief systems that are familiar to them. In a practical and humanistic sense, however, it must be recognized and accepted that a sensitive, culturally aware, skilled and mature person, regardless of ethnic background, can, must, and will teach American youngsters of diversity, and do it well. To have aides from the community becomes a bonus and adds to the potential for identification and for motivation among the children.

And a final note: unless we become expansive in our thinking, as populations shift and technology rushes onward, we will be saddled with thousands of expensive structures that are obsolete or uninhabited. Our investment must not be wasted. School buildings must be constructed today with the idea of community use in mind. They must be flexible, convertible, easily maintained structures. They must be so constructed that teachers and the community can find them useful at once. And they must be so planned that school personnel acting as community aides can have at easy disposal the technical machinery of this electronic and computerized age.

Leadership in the Schools

In the administration of our schools, the democracy we profess by spoken and written words is totally contradicted by facts. The children in the community see and feel this.

Teachers have long attempted to impart information about the founding and furthering of American political liberties. Many have had enough insight into how people learn to try to structure their own classrooms democratically (within the limiting rules of the school and the system), so that children can live that which they have been taught is so great and good. Yet, the schools themselves are not models of democracy in any sense. (Some would have it that that is the way it should be, that there is no intent that knowledge should be passed on at the "whim of the child"; which shows an immense distortion about what *ought* to be going on in a schoolroom.)

For the most part, schools are not democratic in the classrooms, but what is even more obvious to the public, they are not democratic in their administrative relationships. The public must "go through the principal" to talk to a teacher or if Jerome or Jesús is in trouble. At a conference, the public can readily see who runs the institution.

Though the principal or his staff could very well serve a mediating or screening function in order to protect the teachers, it has become obvious to the public that he now serves a controlling function which complicates communication between them and their child's teacher.

The primary function of education involves only the teacher and the children. The administrators, the supervisors, all other attendant personnel should be there for the sole purpose of serving and facilitating that tandem. The teacher should not ask permission of the principal to take a trip, order materials, see a film—do whatever *he* as the immediate and close and intimate helper of the children believes he wants to do. The principal should coordinate the trips, he should distribute materials equitably, he should mediate teacher conflicts, he should research curriculum which he might believe useful for teachers and their children, and he should alert teachers to opportunities and developments; he should *not* make a curriculum, make rules, choose activities, decide upon teacher strategies.

But, just as we see the model administrator as less authoritarian, less in control, more alert to the helper's role for the teachers and the children, so do others, on a nation-wide scale, call for total reexamination; some even to the point of eradicating the position of appointed principal.

In a 1969 article by a classroom teacher in Chicago, read nationwide, the following suggestion was made:

I suggest that the position of the principal assigned by a downtown office as the chief executive of the school be abolished. I also suggest that each school in a large city be run by a faculty council of the experienced teachers of that school; all teachers with ten years of service in the school would be members of the council. Principals, assistant principals, and school administrators would be elected on a part-time basis by the faculty council, leaving much of their day free for the important work of the school, teaching. These people would serve for limited terms. (3)

The writer maintains that such a plan would help to attract and retain better teachers and would cause parents and the community to get actively involved in their children's education. While an intriguing goal, from our own perspective such an idea has little chance of being implemented. However, in some of its aspects it would integrate nicely with our earlier thoughts on teacher groups within each school encountering each other in very frank and open meetings so that an understanding of purposes could be shared.

For the powerless people of the community, such an idea would certainly provide a model of operative democracy which they are constantly told we all live by. It would also offer them increased opportunity to involve themselves with a broader power base at the school. And if we may presume to add to another's thoughts, the people of the community may even wish to form a parent's council (*not* a PTA) which would coordinate its activities with the faculty council. Two bodies (*not* an upper and a lower house) with consultative functions. How exciting is the potential here for neighborhood participation with the teachers of the local schools! In fact, "Community Advisory Boards" have begun to appear in elementary and secondary schools around the country. Administrators are finding them most helpful in spreading the base of responsibility for school and community guidelines and in consultation on matters which have the potential for controversy.

Those principals who currently are attempting to stimulate teachers in their schools and to release the creative imaginations of some of their more tradition-bound pedagogues, have a terrifying task at present: They have many teachers who are caught in an authoritarian maze; a large share of the public believes in the strong hand of the ruler; social research indicates that no one learns in an atmosphere of coercion; and many professional educators in positions of leadership have become irretrievably divorced from the notion that the primary and vital personalities in learning are the learner and the teacher. The contradictions in the enlightened principal's job are enormous.

And, whether elected by the faculty they are to guide, or appointed by the Board or their designates, it seems apparent that principals of today must heed the calls of their community. Regardless of the restrictiveness of their previous ideas of leadership, today's intricate balances require a sharing of power and an inclusion of all elements of education: faculty, students, community, in the processes of decision-making. The principal, like the teacher, is really a worker in a community and must be reactive to that community and to its needs. He must "lead" less and feel, relate, interact, and be available more. The revolution in public education must include a rebirth of the concepts of democratic leadership.

Notes   1. Carkhuff, Robert R., and Bernard G. Berenson. *Beyond Counseling and Therapy*. New York: Holt, 1967, p. 291.

2. Halpern, Ray. "Tactics for Integration—The Berkeley Plan." *Saturday Review,* December 21, 1968, pp. 47ff.

3. Silverman, Joseph. "A Simple Suggestion." *Changing Education,* a publication of the American Federation of Teachers, Washington, D.C., 3, 4, Winter 1969, pp. 37–39. Reprinted by permission.

4. Trubowitz, Sidney. *A Handbook for Teaching in the Ghetto School.* Chicago: Quadrangle Books, Inc., 1968, p. 139. Reprinted by permission.

Part Four

The Beginning

Chapter Ten

Who Are the Powerless?

A Synthesis

Face of Poverty

No one can communicate to you
The substance of poverty
Can tell you either the shape,
Or the depth,
Or the breadth
Of poverty—
Until you have lived with her intimately.

No one can guide your fingers
Over the rims of her eye sockets,
Over her hollow cheeks—
Until perhaps one day
In your wife's once pretty face
You see the lines of poverty;
Until you feel
On her now skinny body,
The protruding bones,
The barely covered ribs,
The shrunken breasts of poverty.

Poverty can be a stranger
In a far-off land:
An alien face
Briefly glimpsed in a newsreel,
An empty rice bowl
In a skinny brown hand,
Until one bleak day
You look out the window—
And poverty is the squatter
In your own backyard.

Lucy Smith. Portion of "Face of Poverty"
by Lucy Smith from New Negro Poets:
U.S.A., *edited by Langston Hughes.*
Copyright © 1964 by Langston Hughes.
Reprinted by permission of Indiana
University Press.

The poor of America have been helpless to alter their own conditions of life. They have been characterized by a poverty of spirit and of self-esteem as well as economic dependence. The ongoing, serialized tragedy is just now beginning to be examined with more than bombast and political propaganda.

To be *different* in America has been to be powerless. Exclusivity and chauvinism have marked the dominant culture. Skin color has something to do with it.

> If you're white,
>   you're all right;
> If you're brown,
>   stick around;
> If you're black,
>   get way back.

But differences in styles of living, ways of believing, language usage—in short, the very uniqueness that characterizes differing cultures—have in the past been held as suspicious, alien, and inferior by the ministers of America's service institutions.

Recently, a person not connected with public education asked me what the point of this book is. "What is your basic message? And what tools do you propose we should provide for the children of the poor to help them to *make it,* however that is defined?"

My primary thesis has been that *the children of America who are poor and different have been characterized by personalities of despair.* The secondary thesis has been that a sense of adequacy, a feeling of goodness about themselves, and an awareness of increased personal power are the tools which must have the highest priority if the poor are to change their condition. And the third major thesis is that the poor must be as much as possible the instruments of their own elevation; to fail to allow for or work toward this would be to deny a basic element of our second thesis.

There is reason to be hopeful about change in our educational institutions. The hope arises from the activities of the young themselves. Incipient power has begun to show among the formerly hopeless; the pride and the self-enhancement that accompany self-promoted change are becoming evident. A rather remarkable power is growing among some of the culturally diverse groups in America—a power which, because of its youth and historical freshness, has yet to be corrupted. A power untainted by coercion of other groups, unmarked by the steady build-up of bureaucratic authoritarianism: a power born of unity, of common purpose, of intense group pride.

Perhaps as we examine carefully the qualities of this emerging power we shall come to a consideration of more germinal meanings of the ideas of societal and individual health, human potential, and the recurring specter of powerlessness. . . .

The most famous of the powerless of our nation have been black people. And it is the blacks who have begun this generation's struggle for personal power. In *Black Rage,* a now nationally known book by two black psychiatrists, it is argued that black people in America can never be free and strong and sound (powerful!) until and unless the black man has the means by which he can protect his family. They note that, traditionally, the black family ". . . is weak and relatively ineffective because the United States sets its hand against black people and by the strength of wealth, size, and number prevents black families from protecting their members." (2) A program to strengthen black families ". . . would include a change in the working of governments so that black people could command that officials serve them, not humiliate them; that policemen protect them, not prey on them." (2) And until the black man perceives that the institutions of America work *for,* not *against,* the protection of his family, he cannot feel that he is truly in control of his life or his destiny; he is a humiliated and powerless man.

Benjamin Scott, a black writer, in *The Coming of the Black Man,* (9) writes a compelling demand for liberation of Americans of African ancestry. Why, he asks, do they want to be called black? Is there something uplifting about defining one's "self" in the world— about establishing one's own sense of identity? For Scott, Black Power is the only way that black people will rise above colonial status in their own native country. And he describes such power as a sense of unity, community, "soul," and self-determination. Until such power is felt, black men remain humiliated and powerless.

Eldridge Cleaver writes about the "low-riders" of Watts in his book, *Soul on Ice.* (1) The cool cats of Watts came to be known as "low-riders." What is there about that term that is endearing to the black movement for status? Is it self-applied? Does it represent significant action by blacks *for* blacks? Is it something applicable to a black man and the black culture? And is it, therefore, somehow strangely uplifting and enhancing? Without the self-identity, the self-initiated movement toward personal control, the black man remains humiliated and powerless.

And what of the Black Students' Union and the Black Panthers? Are these indeed paramilitary, revolutionary groups nihilistically bent upon destruction? Or do they too provide that spark of manhood, of belonging, of identification for the black man? When the Black Panthers describe their function as "policing the police" to see to it that black people get fair treatment, is that not rather closely related to the thesis in *Black Rage* that a man needs to perceive the institutions of his country as protecting, not destroying, his family? And when the Black Students' Union admonishes all young black students not to play football for "the man, 'cause you came to school here to study, not to get exploited," could their deeper motivation have anything to do with ultimately uplifting a personality that has been humiliated and powerless?

The corollary to the drive for personal power among the black activists in society is the drive for relevant education in the schools. If black is indeed beautiful, then black culture and its antecedents and appurtenances must certainly be beautiful topics for study. . . .*

The Chicano and the Puerto Rican have never been slaves in this country. They are powerless because they are different: They are bilingual and basically rural and cooperative in their life styles. Racial prejudice stalks them. They have been the subject of much stereotyping, and they are also quite visible as a minority group. They have been restricted from practicing with pride the culture they know and have been made ashamed of their difference.

The Traditionally Powerless

Their children enter our schools with gentle and respectful timidity, and our schools quickly overpower them with a sense of their inadequacies and their strangeness. They begin a slow death at an early age. . . .

Puerto Ricans in the squalid barrios of the Eastern cities desperately strive to retain and to use their own language. But the schools have obtusely and doggedly insisted upon the use of English alone. Only recently, stirred by pressures from within the communities, have schools encouraged the use of Spanish as a permissible second language for school children to speak.

Chicanos, holding to a more pastoral, accepting, familial, and cooperative cultural style, have found the demands upon them to compete with the Anglo overpowering. They have retreated into their families and neighborhoods, have become taciturn in school, and they seem, to the Anglo world, to lose what spark of life and activeness they had.

---

* For a concise but thorough bibliography of all facets of the black experience in America, see "Men Who Think Black," by Paul M. Smith, Jr., in *The Personnel and Guidance Journal*, May 1970, Vol. 48, #9, pp. 763–766.

But as the blacks have their Panthers, the Chicanos have their Brown Berets. Pride and an uplifting sense of identification mark the Chicanos who have been touched by the Brown Berets. Their goals (described in their handbook) point to their desire to enhance and to support all Chicanos (the name "Chicano" itself, they say, is filled with pride because it is self-taken) through peaceful means if possible, and to protect all Chicanos through whatever means necessary.

Throughout the West and Southwest, Chicanos rally around the new and now militant breed of leaders—the fiery Reies Tijerina (El Tigre) in New Mexico, the magnetic "Corky" Gonzales in Denver, the gentle and charismatic Cesar Chavez in the central California valleys.

Something is happening in Spanish Harlem as well. One energetic Puerto Rican-American VISTA volunteer described the block-organizing, the political action, the tough and dedicated young men and women who are *telling,* not asking, the city fathers what must be initiated if the brown-skinned youngsters of the barrio are to grow to proud and dignified manhood. The Real Great Society is one self-winding group that sparks the drive for pride in Puerto Ricanness.

And in our schools, young people of Mexican ancestry are finding, as did the blacks, that tightly knit and purposeful organization builds the good feelings that lead to confident action. The United Mexican American Students (UMAS) are telling the world that Chicanos are beautiful and magnificent people with a culture that matches anything the Anglo can claim. At UMAS meetings there is a camaraderie and a oneness of purpose that sings with human vibrance and solidarity. Even in their polemics a strange quality of respect and of genuine tenderness softens differences.

As the brown-skinned powerless of this country reach for personal power and pride, that mysterious quality (again, I am repeatedly awed by its intensity), that profound aspect of growth-motivation mentioned earlier, pervades every action and every word. As Chicanos cry "Viva la Raza!" or "Viva la Causa!" the people are listening. . . .*

The American Indian Powerless

"Boastful people cannot become part of a Hopi Village. Only those who desire to live peacefully, to harm no one, are admitted into the religious order of the village life. Not all can be admitted. . . . Peo-

---

* For a sensitive, authentic, and poignant account of the Chicanos in the barrios of East Los Angeles (their history and evolution), read Richard Vasquez' novel, *Chicano* (Doubleday and Company, Inc., Garden City, N.Y., 1970).

ple should not disregard each other. There should be respect for all peoples." (3) This brief excerpt from a statement by a chief and patriarch of the Hopi Indians reveals that, with at least some of the Indians of our land, an awareness of the fabric of true human power existed long before the influence of the white man and the coming of economic and coercive power.

Yet, the Indian in America has remained in wretched poverty, stripped of his close-to-the-earth mode of living, and left unprepared for the cacaphony of American urban demands. He has been indeed among the most traditionally powerless in this country. He has had no freedom to alter or influence his condition. And yet, as with the black and the brown, the red man, too, has begun to stir. The angry spokesmen for the slowly organized Indian legions decry the legendary, fawning "Uncle Tom-a-Hawks." They are resistant to assimilation, proud of themselves and their earthy, cooperative heritage. They are committed to educating themselves, to escaping from the degrading indoctrination of the Bureau schools, to retaining their language and their love of the land.

Reports are increasing of attempts by many Indian tribes or subgroups to "do it for themselves," to provide an education for their own so that they will be prepared to choose their own way of life. For example, in northeastern Arizona, a Navaho Community College, established and controlled by Indians, was founded in 1969. It is open to any Navaho over the age of eighteen, regardless of his earlier schooling.

Robert Roessel, Jr., the first president of the college, very graphically described the reasoning behind a self-run college:

For years the white man's schools—and that's what the Indians call them —have educated the Indianness out of these people, taught the young people that the hogan is dirty, that their parents were ignorant.

The result is a group of bleached Indian youth, who are miserable on the Reservations but rarely learn to adjust when they leave for the big city. They are neither Anglo nor Indian, but just full of self-hatred. (7)

The new school is called by the Indians "dine beolta" (the peoples' school), while the public day schools or the Mission schools were always known as "belagona beolta" (white man's schools). A ten-man Navaho Board of Regents elected from all over the reservation oversees the entire operation of the college. A student is a voting member of the Board. And while vocational courses are among the most in-demand parts of the curriculum, a stirring and uplifting concomitant of the experiment is its influence on the pride of being an

Indian. One young Navaho, Albert Laughter, a Business Education major, seemed to speak for many other people:

Some day, I may sit behind a big desk, with a big job. But no matter how many degrees I have, I want to be able to wear my knot (the traditional Navaho hair style) with pride. I don't want to forget my great-grand-fathers, as other tribes have, and I don't want people to forget that Albert Laughter is a Navaho. (7)

And Roessel (who stepped down after six months as President of the college, in favor of a Navaho) ties this example together rather precisely with earlier themes of this writing when he states: "This is not an either-or situation. We're not urging students either to leave the reservation or to stay. We're just educating them to make an intelligent choice, which is something they've never been offered." (7)

So again the theme recurs. People begin to take action for them-selves—to reach their own destiny—and the power of achievement and of self-dignity is felt. And again this power stirs the imagination and baffles the common-sense notion of what has always been ac-cepted as right and as good and as powerful. Is there indeed some-thing strangely *more* powerful about the active and assertive Indian of today than there is about our obviously and all-too-well-known powerful of the middle-class?

Others Who Are Powerless

In the earliest chapters of this book, passing reference was made to the poor of America who are white but who are also engaged in the uphill struggle for a sense of personal power. White-skinned Americans have generally found that assimilation into the wider culture, both in society at large and in our schools, has been quite readily achieved so long as residuals from their old-world (usually European) cultures have been deemphasized. Some Americans, either by deep economic poverty or by conscious decision, have not been assimilated despite their whiteness. These include the rural whites from Appalachia and other isolated communities, the religious sects who live in ghettoized urban centers, and others whose old-world culture remained so pervasive that the American culture never quite got in. Some who seem to fall into this last category include the nonwhite, Oriental American, who has small numbers of poor, but within whose membership we find some of the poorest (and most powerless) of Americans.

To be answered completely, the question which begins this chapter —Who are the powerless?—must include an analysis of these subgroups who are not quite so visible on America's broad landscape. And yet, they too send their children to our schools, and their children come with personalities of despair. It is our task to understand them and their attitudes if we are to help them. And we must be able to see how their powerlessness is all of a piece with the powerlessness of those groups to whom we have devoted much of this writing.

A job-placement counselor for the California State Department of Employment, working out of an office that serviced every ethnic and cultural minority as well as poor whites, gave this bit of insight:

The Rural-White Powerless

> The white poor have none of the unity of neighborhood or identity that the black or Chicano poor have. The white Anglo does not come to the big city and find relatives or soul brothers. *He* comes to the food closet to get free food—while the black poor tend to help each other. The white poor make excuses for having to receive help: "When my check comes in, I'll. . . ." or "My arm has been bad, but. . . ."
>
> Illegitimacy among the white poor is so much more disgraceful. They are so completely caught up in the Protestant ethic. In the black community, an aunt or a grandmother takes over. The white mother has never been able to take over or to be the stoic woman going it alone the way the black mothers have.
>
> Yet, the white men *are* going to make it on their own. Welfare is demeaning to them—*it* is for the blacks or the Chicanos. If you work hard you will make it—still dominates the white man's belief system. In fact, the whites have "no excuse" from their view of it, so they look for a scapegoat. And often it is the blacks. I've found more prejudice about race and color among the white poor than in any other white stratum.

Now while the poor white man with great gusto and bravado announces to the world that he can make it alone, in the deeper tissues of his makeup, he is a lonely, defeated, pathetic, hollow person. Precisely *because* they perceive themselves as having no excuse, the poor whites of America (racially, the largest group of poor) find their powerlessness a deeply personal and demeaning shortcoming. They boast of changes of luck, or complain about the blacks' getting the government programs—and they are obsessed with their own personal sense of inferiority. But why are the whites of this country who are poor made to feel so helpless, so inferior, so powerless?

VISTA workers, assigned to help the poor in this country, have brought some disturbing analyses to the situation. Writing in *VISTA Volunteer,* the publication of the organization, Padraic Kennedy, the 1969 Acting Director, tells us:

VISTA Volunteers learn by living with people who are different—different in their life styles and different in that *poverty* has robbed them of their right to make the choices that determine their future.

. . . Too many people respond to the problems of the poor with the cliche, "We made it on our own, why can't they?" "We" can be any one of many groups—the immigrants of fifty years ago—the original immigrants who came over a hundred and fifty years ago. "They" are invariably the ethnic groups still identified, as groups, with poverty. The implication is that all of the first groups arrived, worked hard, and earned suburban plots and large-screen TV sets.

But the deeper implication is that the current poor are different; they are not willing to work hard enough. (5)

This attitude of the affluent majority (the middle class) penetrates deeply into the outlooks of those in poverty, and it adds to their defeat and increases their powerlessness. The attitude, if we are willing to face it, is a rejection of difference—an intolerance of differently paced cultures or styles of living. Whiteness, in the final analysis, cannot of itself overcome the prejudice against behavioral or cultural diversity. . . .

Typical of the white poor of America are the much-publicized people of Appalachia. What has happened to them and where are they today? What power have the Appalachian poor who have migrated to the cities been able to assume? Another VISTA member helps us to answer these questions. A young woman who worked as a Volunteer among the Appalachians writes:

Drive back up into the hills of Appalachia and study some of America's earliest immigrants—White—Anglo-Saxon—Protestant-poor. In the American equation of money equals success, many of the hill people are failures.

. . . There is little understanding of them as a people disoriented, desperately in need of recognition as individuals in a society where you have to have something to sell before you are given respect.

. . . The [Appalachian] region is spoken of by Appalachian writers in terms of passion and myth. Jess Stuart, in an article in *Mountain Life and Work*, speaks of Appalachian voices: "They are the world's best poets who have never written a line and the world's best story tellers who have never written a story."

. . . [Yet] people from all stations of life in Appalachia seek opportunity elsewhere. Many of those who leave the hills for the northern cities are those whose attachment to the land is the strongest, who leave only out of desperation. They have been crowded out by their own high birth rate, by the deterioration of small farms on unfertile soil, by the end of jobs in the coal mines or jobs which were created by the coal industry, and by the higher cost of living.

There is no place for them in Appalachia. There is no place for them in the northern cities.

. . . In city ghettos [they] are described by some social workers as suspicious. . . . An impersonal sense of social responsibility is not part of many Southern Appalachians' culture. You owe your kin loyalty and aid. It does not occur to you that some total stranger, an agency, would be concerned. For a stranger to assume responsibility is offensive; it implies that you are not doing your duty by your family.

. . . [But the Appalachian] has much to offer as a human being. . . . [There] is an unusual sensitivity and innate courtesy. There is a quiet graciousness. There is a refreshing, unhurried enjoyment of small tasks. It takes time to get to know the Appalachian. What the Appalachian has to give has much to do with time. (10)

Implicit in this sensitive description is the powerlessness felt by the white poor from Appalachia as their lives touch the superior attitudes of those of America who have made it. Imagine the unbelievable shame a little child from the hills has felt as she has been exposed in our urban schools to the standardized processes of our public education. Imagine her sense of difference and worthlessness as she has absorbed the rather narrow and homogenizing message our institutions have broadcast.

And yet, the die is cast . . . as the black powerless, the brown powerless, and the red powerless organize themselves into meaningful activity—as their prospects rise in direct relation to their emerging pride—so must the white powerless join the struggle toward personal power. So must the white powerless find the beauty that sings in their cultural style of living. So must the white powerless find the self-enhancement that comes from believing in one's own goodness and rightness.

The Irish and Jewish Powerless

Although it may be hard to believe, there are Americans today resigned to inferior status who are white and urbanized. They have been handicapped because they are different.

Irish Catholics have always been a minority group in America. In Boston, on the South Side, they were in the majority. Their people were the policemen, the firemen, the clergy, and the politicians. Interestingly, many who "worked hard and made it" and moved out to greener suburbs tend today to have a certain nostalgia for "Old

Southie," but also to forget the Irish brothers and sisters who remain there in fading squalor.

South Boston is only one area where the old-culture Irish linger on, and yet, the statement of one of its life-long residents speaks for the Irish poor everywhere:

The Irish particularly, have a strange pride about poverty. A needy mother is usually ashamed to receive hand-outs or go on welfare, even though she has a child out of school because he doesn't have shoes. On the other hand, she is proud if a boy leaves school to help support the family. (8)

We can see here an interesting parallel with the white poor who came to the Employment Department unwilling to publicly admit their need. But, at least in South Boston, young widowed or husbandless mothers are overcoming the traditional Irish resistance to public support. More and more Irish are having to admit they are poor and are being represented now on the rolls of Aid for Families with Dependent Children.

Why are some Irish Catholics still powerless in America? Why do those who cling to a style of living which brought them great fulfillment and family closeness—a colorful and cultural heritage of the past—why are they powerless to maintain some semblance of control over their lives? That very tenacity, that unwillingness to become a "middle-class American," may be the very thing that is doing them in.

And what of the Jewish who are powerless? Can such an education-oriented, apparently affluent, traditionally achieving cultural group have any significant numbers of poor? Paradoxically, yes. In fact, just a few years ago, powerlessness was a political and economic reality for the majority of Jews in America. Interestingly, though, psychological powerlessness had not stricken many Jews in this country; the strong sense of ethnic and cultural identity and a certain unity bred of persecution had combined to make them clannish and self-supporting. As with the old-world Chinese, as long as you did not allow the new culture to take you over, you could maintain a pride in yourself *for* what you were. But today, as assimilation and middle-classness continue to dominate every means of communication and all the publicly extolled interrelationships, the Jews who cling to traditional cultural attitudes are finding themselves increasingly powerless.

An extreme example of Jews who are poor in America is the Hasidic Jews who live largely in the Williamsburg section of Brooklyn. Ultra-orthodox in their religion and restrictive living patterns, they came to the United States to escape persecution and to be allowed to retain their deeply traditional ways. They do retain those ways—indeed, they prize education and learning, but largely it is the religious study, the strict emphasis on learning the Torah, the prayers, and Jewish law which they exalt—and their ways do not prepare them to participate in the economy of mainstream America.

Many Hasidic Jews live in or near poverty in America. Their customs and religious values are inextricably woven into the fabric of their lives. They will not work on Friday afternoons or Saturdays, and few employers need them on Sundays. Parents still are matchmakers for their children and marriages are arranged by the families. The government resists giving them antipoverty money, claiming that the entire problem is self-imposed.

Non-Hasidic Jews who retain their orthodox ways also find themselves outside the circle of acceptance in middle-class America. Their sense of difference, imposed as it is from an outside, manifestly superior major culture, acts to demean them and their customs. Powerlessness invades their thinking and believing patterns and they begin to doubt their own way. . . .

Langston Hughes, the Negro poet, paid personal tribute to the powerless Jews of this country. Paraphrasing his earlier poem, "Dream Deferred," he wrote:

> Sometimes I think
>   Jews must have heard
> the music of a
>   dream deferred. (4)

The Oriental Powerless

Also traditionally powerless in America, though it is often camouflaged, are citizens of Oriental ancestry. True, there is a cultural heritage—if the children are permitted exposure to it despite our pervasive mainstream culture—which includes a reverence for learning and family fealty. But because of the powerful influence of our middle-class, dominant cultural emphasis, the young, American-born Oriental is becoming ashamed of his ancestors and their traditional way of life. Some Orientals make it despite immediate racial identity, but they become middle-class Americans and are Oriental only in their features.

The little-known but penetrating story of the Chinese-American and his struggle with the narrowness of the American scene is told, again by a VISTA Volunteer. In an article called "On Being Chinese in San Francisco," she writes:

. . . When they holler "boy" in Chinatown, the face which turns is yellow, not black. . . .

Over sixty thousand people live in San Francisco's Chinatown. Twenty-five percent of them live below the city's poverty level of four thousand dollars a year.

For over one hundred years, the Chinese have been our most conspicuous immigrant. Their appearance was as distinctive as Oriental culture, customs, dress and language could make it. They withdrew into themselves, unwilling to sacrifice ancient traditions to live the American life style.

They were persecuted because they were different, but they survived. . . . Nothing was more different to American life than the Chinaman. He did everything backwards. His surname came first. He read from right to left and front to back. When he thought, he scratched his foot instead of his head. The Chinaman shaved the hair from his face, but let it grow in a pig tail down his back (required by old Chinese law). He wore loose-flowing robes, and often went barefoot. . . .

The Chinese existed totally apart and, because of this, the white man mistrusted him. He was the mysterious stranger. . . .

Like the old Christian crusaders, the white man set out to purge the yellow peril. . . . Chinese were hanged, stoned, assaulted, and robbed. Extermination became so commonplace, it was seldom printed in the newspaper. Not to stand a Chinaman's Chance was the watchword of the era. . . .

America. A land of English-speaking people where blonde-headed Dick and Jane watched Spot run. Where as school children they help Washington cross the Delaware and coolies dig ditches. . . . It is beautiful for spacious skies, the land of the free and the brave. It is very different from home. . . .

[The Chinese immigrant] knew America didn't want him; he didn't want America. What culture he absorbed was superfluous and expedient. . . .

Today's Chinese youngster is a cultural hybrid. He must be a Chinese but he wants to be an American. He is a most rejected man. . . . what does he care for ancient prayers and fantan? Suffocating in the womb, he is safe and warm and angry. . . .

He knows he is poor, and he doesn't want to be. He wants to eat steak, not rice. He wants to wear cashmere. He wants a home with three bedrooms and a private bath. . . .

But as fast as the acculturated leave, others move in. . . . Unable to make a living in Hong Kong, they cross the seas to the land of golden opportunity. . . .

Chinatown is again becoming a ghetto of immigrants, old and new. Its boundary is a state of mind, a psychological law which forbids moving out. Its gate is firmly locked by tradition. Because they are different, the immigrants cannot succeed in a life so unlike their own. (12)

The press has begun to show an awareness of the plight of the yellow man in America (San Francisco's Chinatown is estimated to have a population density second only to Harlem's). We can suddenly discover a new militancy, a new awakening among Orientals. (6) Chinese militants (much like the black and the Chicano groups) have aimed their sights at police harassment, but there is evidence that demands in the schools for "yellow people to remain yellow" is also on the rise.

One leader of the movement, a student at San Francisco State College, said it this way: "The idea . . . is to rediscover our identity rather than to merge with white Anglo-Saxon Americans. . . . We want to redefine *American* in terms of the history of the Chinese, Japanese, and Filipinos in America." (6)

Recently, a young Nisei (that is, born in the U.S. to Japanese immigrants) told me that he was involved with a group of Orientals (all Orientals, not just Chinese or Japanese) in the Los Angeles area, who were intent upon sensitizing their people to their right to love and respect their own language and culture, and yet to live in human comfort in America. "We're sick of having to be white to live right," he said. "Sure the black man may have shown us it can be done, but today all the nonwhite people of this country are demanding their due. Black Power has given black people some pride. Well, wake up America, here comes Yellow Power!"

Yes, to live a life of marked, fundamental difference in America is to find yourself in an increasingly restrictive atmosphere that makes you powerless to have impact on your existence. And the children of the powerless who come to our schools have been described here without, in most instances, direct indication of the in-school aspects of their various cultural attitudes. But I strongly feel that those detailed aspects are not of primary significance; what is significant is that the children of culturally diverse parents *will be* culturally diverse. What is of primary significance is that our teachers must not only recognize that fact, but exalt that diversity, approach it as the major curricular force in our programs. If the teachers' attitudes can be expansive and appreciative, then the powerless children in their classes will feel the incipient pride in knowing that they are bright and beautiful young people. . . .

The Middle-Class Powerless

We have asked if a new and unknown kind of power may indeed be arising through the energy and activity of the emerging poor. Many perplexing thoughts are raised by that question.

It is possible that, in their assumption of status and place, middle-class Americans, the traditional holders of power, have ceased to live by the tenets which gave them power. A spiritual lethargy born of complacency is perhaps now beginning to mark the patterns of middle-class activity. Perhaps over the long haul of affluent living it has come to seem easier to command and coerce than to cooperate and enhance. These patterns certainly appear to receive the support of the citizenry when applied in our public schools.*

If the middle class has indeed begun to lose the spark of creativity or freshness that long has continued to provide it with a sense of personal power, and if the exclusivity which has pervaded this sub-culture's attainment and protection of affluence continues, then I would have to predict that its power would begin to decline. But there is even more which is perplexing and in need of clarification.

If, through the years of formal slavery and the subsequent century of cultural chauvinism, groups of American minorities have been degraded, humiliated, and kept powerless, someone or some group must have been the oppressors. Specifics are difficult, but in general, the dominant American middle-class culture has been the oppressor. And sadly, we have developed an oppressor's character. If we ask what effect the relentless and inscrutable domination by one people over another can have upon those who are the dominant, the answer appears to be that it corrupts them. . . .

That mysterious reverence that I have felt for the energy and the erupting power of the culturally diverse in this nation is explained in part by the purity of their emerging strength: it has never been a dominating kind of power, nor a humiliating and chauvinistic power.

It is my contention here that as demeaning as it can be to a people to suffer slavery and oppression, in the final reckoning it is even more debasing to be the oppressor. Those who have been the controllers and the coercers have suffered the loss of the deepest of the elements of human power, a sense of justice, of the humanity of all people, of the more germinal values of man's existence. The oppressed have been weakened by their debasement and continued powerlessness, and yet, their sense of community, of love for each other, of "soul,"

---

* I do not wish to suggest that parents of the typically powerless, the minorities, the different of America, are, as a group, any more alert to the freeing and enhancing approaches to education than are the typical middle-class parents. The impact of *reading, writing,* and *arithmetic,* and of strict discipline, have been so powerful as desired goals, so pervasive as the "ends" of education in our society, that many minority parents wait with their adrenalin flowing for the results of the latest standardized achievement test. And even more, they will, very often, explode with anger at the public school teacher who is not giving their children "the skills they will need to make it." That those skills mean nothing unless accompanied by insights on *how* to learn and feelings that one is able to learn, is often lost on them completely.

What I do suggest is that many of the more active youth of today, rising as they are from their state of powerlessness, are willing to "use" the current system to achieve the tools that will give them a better chance to change that system.

of commitment to life have grown and expanded. The oppressors
have been the economically affluent and the psychologically in-
control, but in their narrowness of cultural tolerance they have lost
much of the joy of living.

Power is the ability to control one's destiny. We all are restricted
and limited in our power—we are social beings. But some have had
relatively more power, historically and in recent times, than others.
When we consider the deeper nature of a positive, durable power, we
must ask: Who are, indeed, the powerless?

That the children of today's poor may feel the power that some of **Programs for**
their elders are demanding, our schools must reconstitute their edu- **Power**
cational menu. Power and pride come from self-initiated investigations and personally perceived accomplishments. We have described
programs and attitudes which can bring such power; they are growing
in number, and, we hope, the awareness of their need is reaching our
formal educational structure.

But, as we have written earlier, those in positions of power must
willingly relinquish some of it if the emerging poor are to have a
chance to try it for themselves. If programs are created by the presently powerful that include the activities and the perspectives of the
powerless, if the imaginative know-how of those with experience can
be applied to programs for the new and the different in our society, if
through the cooperation of the affluent and the emerging, new tolerance can be gained for diverse attitudes and beliefs—only if all these
conditions are planned for by the majority, only then can disruption
and chaos be averted. Historically, our educational institutions have
been powerful forces in the process of cultural continuity. What they
must begin to recognize today is how remarkably more complex than
we realized are America's several cultures, and how desperately
urgent is our need to pass on to our young the legitimacy of all of
them.

We have written about *a curriculum that might be*. It must be   *A Review*
based upon a psychological, a humanistic model: It must grow out
of the nature and the needs of the learner. It cannot be imposed from
the outside by some powerful, distant board or by sanctuaried
theoreticians.

We have proposed that textbooks be made more relevant, more a
part of the lives and worlds of the learners. We have cited examples
of personalized and even personally created books.

We have argued for the appreciation of the language styles children know and for an end to the degradation children feel when told that their only way of speaking is wrong. Teaching Standard English as a second language may be the key to this.

We have proposed intense programs of human relations in our schools, giving due to the affective aspect of the curriculum. Children must be able to express their feelings as well as their ideas. Bull sessions or weekly class meetings may go a long way to unify a class into a group.

We have described instances where children have learned best from their peers. We must plan for this in our public schools, encouraging communication among students, and putting an end to our legacy of "silence is golden."

We have proposed a more divergent and creative structure for our classrooms. Children of little power need many opportunities to think expansively, to stretch their imaginations, to discover and to be surprised at their own insights.

A major proposal of ours concerns the role of the teacher as a facilitator of learning experiences for the young: a guide and a helper of children, not a teller and a controller. Ways to develop facilitators in our schools include: a more intensified and personalized (perhaps live-in) approach to teacher education; a more applied teacher-education curriculum, which encourages on-site experiences, in-community classes and meetings, simultaneous theory-and-practice exposures; a planned exposure to the deeper feelings a teacher-to-be has, through small encounter groups and more intimate interaction with peers and professors; similar deep-reaching experiences for teachers in service and for administrators as well; a more penetrating exposure to the people of diversity whom young teachers will be confronting, through intense sociological and psychological study of the diverse cultures among America's minorities, and of the culture of poverty.

Facilitators also must deeply and honestly care about their learners, who when they feel cared for will dare to try. They must expect and encourage their children to do things for themselves, to discover new things, to explore, to examine, to experiment. And they must help to create an atmosphere that is nonjudgmental. When the powerless begin to feel the strength of self-evaluation, they become creative and assertive about their activities.

Teachers who wish to be true facilitators to their culturally diverse children may have to become teachers-in-a-community, where their work becomes a more unified, holistic encounter with an entire environment than subject-matter teaching in a single classroom. The teacher-as-facilitator may need to use community aides, and may need to become a community aide, and may find a completely new role as the power begins to shift away from a single authority, a principal, and becomes shared by teachers, students, and community.

Educating the powerless is an intricate task and may require massive overhaul of our public structures, of our teacher education programs, of our entire way of looking at subject matter and at learners. The change has already begun, and is illustrated by several programs mentioned earlier—some of which have been self-started and self-engineered by the emerging poor: The Navahos in northeastern Arizona have reached for personal power through their self-initiated, self-run community college. At the Rough Rock Demonstration School in Arizona the entire Navaho boarding school is administered by Indians—and parents are paid as aides and attend adult education classes. The Black Students' Unions in colleges and universities throughout the country have influenced the creation of departments of Afro-American Studies as centers of identification for Americans of African ancestry. The United Mexican-American Students have enjoined other members of La Raza to feel the pride of their people and their culture.

Programs at Fordham, Syracuse, Pittsburgh, and other institutions, have begun to initiate on-site and interactive teacher education experiences. The community has become active (and will become more so) in the operation and development of their local public schools. Community aides and teachers of the same cultural background as the school population are increasingly apparent in our local schools. Child-centered and culturally diverse approaches are being encouraged and instituted with public school children in such places as Berkeley and Philadelphia. The School Without Walls, in Philadelphia, is a successful venture into outside-the-classroom approaches to relevancy for today's curriculum. Papago Indian children, besides writing their own books, find their parents tutoring, and working alongside the teachers.

Teacher education is just now beginning to experiment with deeply sensitizing encounter experiences in bringing teachers-to-be to an awareness of their own personalities and the impact they have on their children.

Quite exciting, and though not American, perhaps one of the most complete examples of the kind of education we have been recommending is the children-centered programs currently operating in one third of England's primary schools. This program catches the essence of what I believe is needed for the children of powerlessness in America: the British "classrooms alive with chaos." *Life* magazine, describing this program in the spring of 1969, quoted one young child who suggested that school should be made ". . . so we can walk around because we were born free." (11)

A Beginning   In educating the powerless, America must examine her practices . . . and her destiny. But because programs for power will provide just as much as the ministers of those programs permit, it is ultimately with the teachers and their attitudes that the elimination of inferiority and the powerlessness of cultural difference rests.

Our writing closes with a final challenge, a challenge to the deeper meaning of American patriotism and national pride. Can our schools continue to apply the delicate and narrow tolerance for behavioral and cultural styles that have dominated them in the past? Or can we live up to our original, prophetic destiny as a land of cultural diversity and of educational opportunity for all? Can all American children receive valuable educations in our public schools while retaining and cherishing their own identities, pride in themselves, the uniqueness of their cultures, and a sense of control or power over their own destinies? This is our challenge and our opportunity. Perhaps a beginning has been made. . . .

Notes   1. Cleaver, Eldridge. *Soul on Ice*. New York: McGraw-Hill, 1968.

2. Grier, William H., and Price M. Cobbs. *Black Rage*. New York: Bantam Books, 1969, p. 71.

3. Hermequaftewa, Andrew. "The Hopi Way of Life is the Way of Peace." From a tape-recorded interview with the Bluebird Chief of the Hopi Village of Shungopavi, 1968.

4. Hughes, Langston. From the poem "Likewise," in *The Langston Hughes Reader*. New York: George Braziller, Inc., 1958, pp. 121–122. Reprinted by permission of Harold Ober Associates, Incorporated. Copyright 1951 by Langston Hughes.

5. Kennedy, Padraic. "On Being Different." *VISTA Volunteer*, 5, 2, February 1969, p. 3. Reprinted by permission of the author and publisher.

6. Lamott, Kenneth. "The Awakening of Chinatown." *West Magazine*, The Los Angeles Times, January 4, 1970, pp. 7–14.

7. Mathews, Linda. "Navahos Chart Educational Path." *Los Angeles Times,* June 1, 1969. Copyright 1969 by the Los Angeles Times. Reprinted by permission.

8. Murphy, Betty. "On Being Irish in Boston." *VISTA Volunteer,* 5, 2, February 1969, pp. 10–16.

9. Scott, Benjamin. *The Coming of the Black Man*. Boston: Beacon, 1969.

10. Urvant, Ellen. "On Being from the Hills of Appalachia." *VISTA Volunteer,* 5, 2, February 1969, pp. 4–8. Reprinted by permission of the publisher and author.

11. Villet, Barbara. "The Children Want Classrooms Alive with Chaos." *Life,* April 11, 1969, pp. 50ff.

12. Wilansky, Eileen. "On Being Chinese in San Francisco." *VISTA Volunteer,* 5, 2, February 1969, pp. 18–22. Reprinted by permission of the publisher and author.

Index